D1227109

TEACHING HISTORY WITH BIG IDEAS

CASES OF AMBITIOUS TEACHERS

Edited by
S. G. Grant and Jill M. Gradwell

ROWMAN & LITTLEFIELD EDUCATION
A division of
ROWMAN & LITTLEFIELD PUBLISHERS, INC.
Lanham • New York • Toronto • Plymouth, UK

Published by Rowman & Littlefield Education
A division of Rowman & Littlefield Publishers, Inc.
A wholly owned subsidary of The Rowman & Littlefield Publishing Group, Inc.
4501 Forbes Boulevard, Suite 200, Lanham, Maryland 20706
http://www.rowmaneducation.com

Estover Road, Plymouth PL6 7PY, United Kingdom

Copyright © 2010 by S. G. Grant and Jill M. Gradwell

All rights reserved. No part of this book may be reproduced in any form or by any electronic or mechanical means, including information storage and retrieval systems, without written permission from the publisher, except by a reviewer who may quote passages in a review.

British Library Cataloguing in Publication Information Available

Library of Congress Cataloging-in-Publication Data

Teaching history with big ideas : cases of ambitious teachers / edited by S.G. Grant and Jill M. Gradwell.
    p. cm.
  Includes bibliographical references and index.
  ISBN 978-1-60709-765-5 (cloth : alk. paper) — ISBN 978-1-60709-766-2 (pbk. : alk. paper) — ISBN 978-1-60709-767-9 (electronic)
  1. History—Study and teaching (Secondary)—Case studies. 2. Curriculum planning. I. Grant, S. G. II. Gradwell, Jill M., 1969-
  D16.2.T395 2010
  907.1'2—dc22

                                                                2010005352

∞™ The paper used in this publication meets the minimum requirements of American National Standard for Information Sciences—Permanence of Paper for Printed Library Materials, ANSI/NISO Z39.48-1992.

Printed in the United States of America

SEP 2 1 2010

CONTENTS

PREFACE

The standard complaint among educators of social studies teachers is that teachers resist their progressive instructional suggestions. The standard complaint among social studies teachers is that educators' suggestions flop in their classrooms. Teacher educators view teachers as obstinate and conservative; teachers view teacher educators as naïve and out of touch. Or so the story goes.

Like most stories, this one represents at least some measure of reality. Teachers, both preservice and practicing, react negatively to glib pronouncements that their traditional approaches are all wrong and that turning every assignment into a cooperative learning activity guarantees success. On the other side, teacher educators become vexed when their ideas are rejected out of hand in favor of activities that they know will not reach all students. Having lived on each side of this divide, both editors of this volume can recount any number of examples of mistrust and miscommunication between classroom teachers and university academics.

Reality, however, is always more complex than the stories we tell. Teachers and academics may see some things differently, but not all. In fact, in a small study that we conducted, the teacher and university respondents demonstrated a high degree of agreement about the kinds of assessments that best measure students' historical knowledge and understanding. The two groups were not in sync on everything, but the thrust of what they did agree on—that measures of student learning can and ought to be more challenging—is no small thing.

So the story of how teachers and teacher educators view each other and schooling is complex. One point that seems beyond dispute, however, is that if teachers are going to teach in ambitious ways, then they need to see what that kind of teaching looks like.

For many years, social studies academics focused on the intellectual foundations of the field. Those university professors who conducted empirical studies tended to focus on the mean—the patterns that surfaced in typical classrooms. These pieces, while useful, did little to either inspire or give guidance to classroom teachers who wanted to teach more ambitiously. Told that they needed to teach in richer and more engaging fashion, teachers rightly asked, "What does that look like?"

That question largely went unanswered until recently. For the last twenty years or so, researchers have shifted some of their attention away from typical teachers and directed it toward exemplary teachers. That effort has not resulted in a singular view—one set of knowledge and skills, one set of professional dispositions, one set of instructional practices. Good teaching is complex and manifests in any number of ways. So while researchers may have failed to produce a single, coherent view of good teaching, they succeeded in putting forward rich and accessible accounts of what good teaching looks like.

Missing from the literature on good teaching, however, have been accounts written by teachers themselves. It is one thing for researchers to document the decisions, challenges, and twists teachers negotiate as they construct and reconstruct their instructional practices to better serve all their students; it is quite another to see those decisions, challenges, and twists described and analyzed by the teachers involved. Of course, neither researcher-observer nor teacher-participant owns the truth of any classroom interaction—after all, students are only rarely given a chance to speak for themselves. But with the addition of the teacher-authored cases in this book, the story of ambitious teaching is now being told from a different set of perspectives.

We use the term "ambitious teaching" deliberately. Although there is no unitary theory of good teaching, we offer the construct of ambitious teaching as a means of capturing the key themes in the extant literature. Those themes, in our view, translate into three kinds of knowledge about subject matter, students, and the teaching context that ambitious teachers hold. Ambitious teachers (1) know their subject matter well and see within it the potential to enrich their students' lives; (2) know their students well, which includes understanding the kinds of lives their students lead, how these youngsters think about and perceive the world, and that they are far more capable than they and most others believe them to be; and (3) know how to create the necessary space for themselves and their students in environments in which others (e.g., administrators, other teachers) may not appreciate their efforts. Ambitious teachers deeply understand their subject matter and they actively seek ways to connect that subject matter with the lived experiences of their students. They often do so, however, while facing contextual factors (e.g., state curricula, state tests, unsupportive administrators and colleagues) that may push them in different directions.

Defined in this fashion, ambitious teaching is less about the instructional practices a teacher uses than it is about what a teacher knows and how she or he interacts with ideas, with students, and with the conditions of schooling. To make ambitious teaching more tangible, however, we have been teaching our prospective and practicing teachers to develop big ideas for the history units they teach. A big idea is a question or generalization that is intellectually honest and is cast in a manner that should appeal to students. For example, the question "What does it mean to be civilized?" has been debated by adults for hundreds of years, yet it is equally intriguing to children because they are so often accused of being otherwise. Big idea units, then, function as a representation of what ambitious teachers know about their subject matter, about their students, and about the local context in which they work.

Because teaching history with big ideas is no simple thing, we thought it useful to ask a group of our former students to think and write about their experiences. Our chapters introduce and conclude the book, but it is the teacher-authored cases that make the real contribution to the field. Representing a range of teaching experiences, school contexts, grade levels, and subjects taught, this group offers a powerful set of insights into the problems and possibilities of teaching ambitiously. We have learned a lot from working with these folks; we expect you will too.

Together, we offer our greatest thanks and appreciation to our teacher-colleagues: Andrew Beiter, Mary Beth Bruce, Tricia Davis, Julie Doyle, Sarah Foels, Joseph Karb, Michael Meyer, and Megan Sampson. Writing is no easy chore—even if (or maybe especially because) one is writing about one's own practice. The early enthusiasm with which we all began this project faded some as chapter drafts were written, rewritten, and then rewritten again. Through it all, however, we could not have been more pleased with the thought, care, and diligence each author gave to her or his chapter. The extra effort clearly shows.

Beyond our teacher-colleagues, Jill Gradwell would like to thank S. G. Grant for introducing her to big idea teaching in a way that inspired her to pass along this approach to the many teachers she has interacted with throughout the years. Without his insight into the world of ambitious teaching, this project would never have been undertaken and completed. Jill would also like to thank her colleagues at Buffalo State College and the generous support of the Dr. Nuala McGann Drescher Leave Program, which created the necessary space to work on this vast project. Jill is especially grateful for all the love, support, and most of all, the patience she received from her husband, Tom, her three boys, Camden, Kellen, and Declan, and her extended family while she was engaged in this work.

S. G. Grant would first like to thank Jill Gradwell. He has benefitted from their collaboration on this book and the studies before it in ways far too numerous to count. Her thoughtfulness, patience, and determination to get our ideas right has been a cornerstone of our work together. In addition, he would like to thank the many students and colleagues and peers he's had the opportunity to talk and work with in his years at the University at Buffalo and now at Binghamton University. In so many ways, the life of an academic is a real luxury; he's been fortunate to be surrounded by people who take teaching and learning seriously. Finally, he would like to thank the family members—Anne, Alexander, and Claire—who keep him grounded in the things that really count.

1

TEACHING HISTORY
WITH BIG IDEAS

S. G. Grant and Jill M. Gradwell

Concerns about the nature of social studies/history[1] teaching refuse to fade: students routinely pan their school history courses and the textbooks used in them (Epstein, 1994; Schug, Todd, & Beery, 1984); teachers routinely employ pedantic materials, instructional strategies, and classroom assessments (Cusick, 1983; Goodlad, 1984; Levstik, 2008); curriculum theorists and policymakers routinely argue over the soul of social studies/history (Evans, 2004; Nash, Crabtree, & Dunn, 2000; Thornton, 2004, 2008); and until recently, social studies academics routinely avoided any serious study of what passes for history teaching and learning in schools (Grant, 2003).

Reports of slight increases in students' performances on National Assessment of Educational Programs (NAEP) history exams (Lapp, Grigg, & Tay-Lim, 2002) fail to allay these concerns. Although the literature base is replete with ideas about how to develop and support rich social studies teaching, advocates for new curriculum standards, for high-stakes testing, for professional development, and for changes in the school day (e.g., block scheduling) have been unable to show a consistently positive effect (Grant, 2003). Good history teachers take no single shape, teach in no single fashion, and assess their efforts with no single measure.

In this book, we share the cases of eight teachers from western New York who vary on as many measures as they cohere. As a group, they differ considerably by age, experience, subjects taught, and school setting. At the same time, they share three important similarities—deep knowledge of and interest in their subject matters, deep knowledge of and concern for the particular students they teach, and teaching assignments in challenging contexts. Building on the works of Shulman (1987), Dewey (1902/1969), Schwab (1978), and Hawkins (1974), Grant (2003, 2005) developed the notion of *ambitious teaching*. While not diminishing the importance of teachers' knowledge of subject matter and students (Shulman, 1987), he argues that the contexts in which teachers work matter, especially as high-stakes testing comes to dominate educational practices. Ambitious teachers, then, (a) know their subject matter well and see within it the potential to enrich their students' lives; (b) know their students well, which includes understanding the kinds of lives their students lead, how these youngsters think about and perceive the world, and that they are far more capable than they and most others believe them to be; and (c) know how to create the necessary space for themselves and their students in environments in which others (e.g., administrators, other teachers) may not appreciate their efforts. Ambitious teachers deeply understand their subject matter and actively seek ways to connect that subject matter with the lived experiences of their students. They often do so, however, while facing contextual factors (e.g., state curricula, state tests, unsupportive administrators and colleagues) that may push them in different directions.

Although the ambitious teaching framework is a powerful analytic construct, practical pedagogical dimensions have gone largely unexamined. Missing from the social studies literature are both practical approaches to realizing ambitious teaching and studies of teachers' efforts to reconstruct their own practices around ambitious teaching principles. The teacher-participants in our project have been using "big ideas" as an instantiation of ambitious teaching. Grant and VanSledright (2006) define a big idea as a question or generalization that helps teachers decide what to teach and how by centering their teaching units in meaty, complex issues that are open to multiple perspectives and interpretations. For example, a question like "Was the American Revolution revolutionary?" gives both teacher and students an engaging place to begin their inquiry into this complex era. The case studies in this book demonstrate the potential for using big ideas with students and in contexts that differ greatly.

BACKGROUND OF THE PROJECT

The principal question driving the project behind this book was "How are ambitious teachers making use of big ideas to teach history?" Initially, we considered crafting the project as a study in which we interviewed the teachers, collected their classroom artifacts, and observed their classes. The more we discussed that traditional research design, however, the more interested we became in an alternative plan in which the teachers told their own stories. Two factors influenced our decision to follow that path. First, although the literature base on ambitious teaching is growing, it is a literature that presents teachers' voices in limited fashion—through the quotes that the researchers select. There is nothing wrong with this approach, but it can lead to a sense that an author's narrative is overwhelming the teachers' perspectives. Wanting to forefront teachers' views was one consideration; wanting to more fully present teachers' experiences was another. Because researchers build their narratives only in part using teachers' words, readers rarely get a rich picture of teachers' thinking as well as their practices. By creating an opportunity whereby teachers could craft their own narratives of thought and action, we expected the ensuing cases to offer a much deeper understanding of pedagogy-in-practice than is typically represented in the extant literature.

As a result, we chose to frame this project around a collection of teacher-written essays, indicative of conceptual teacher research (Cochran-Smith & Lytle, 1993), for an insider's view of the classroom offers a unique lens on understanding teaching and learning, one that an outsider, such as a university researcher, cannot provide (Anderson & Herr, 1999). There are limitations to self-reports, but there are limitations in all forms of research, and the benefits of hearing about the successes and challenges teachers face in their own words are several.

Our invited participant group consisted of three middle school and five high school history teachers (see table 1.1). The eight participants, drawn from classes we have taught at our respective institutions, were selected because they were using big ideas to teach global and/or American history, had varying levels of experience, worked in diverse settings, and were teaching courses with a state-mandated exam. In terms of classroom experience, three are beginning teachers (less than five years of experience), three are experienced teachers (less than ten years of experience), and two are veteran teachers (ten or more years of experience). All of the teachers teach in New York State—three in rural schools, three in suburban schools, and two in city charter schools. We asked each teacher to write a chapter-length reflection of his or her experience teaching one big idea unit of their own design.

For the project, each teacher was instructed to keep a reflective journal to record the planning procedures for the unit they taught, student comments made during unit implementation, successes and failures the teacher sensed were happening, and final thoughts of the overall teaching of the unit. Some teachers made copies of student assessment tasks for reference later when they wrote their essays. As a group, we met three times to introduce the project and check the progress of the teachers' writing. We each read and responded to several drafts of each teacher's essay.

Before we present the teacher-author cases, we first offer a brief overview of the New York State social studies curriculum and testing context. We then describe the two principal constructs that drive this project—ambitious teaching and big idea teaching.

Table 1.1. Characteristics of Teacher-Authors

Name	School Context	Grade(s) Taught	School Subject	Years Experience	Unit Topic
Mike Meyer	Second-ring suburban high school	10	Global History and Geography	5	Ancient African civilizations
Meg Sampson	Urban charter high school	10	Global History and Geography	1	Global history test preparation course
Sarah Foels	Second-ring suburban middle school	8	U.S. History and Geography	3	U.S. Civil War
Andrew Beiter and Joseph Karb	Rural middle school	8	U.S. History and Geography	12 and 9 respectively	Genocide
Mary Beth Bruce	First-ring suburban high school	11	Advanced Placement U.S. History	7	Post–Civil War Reconstruction
Julie Doyle	Rural high school	10	Global History and Geography	3	Imperialism
Tricia Davis	Urban charter high school	9	Global History and Geography	10	Native and European Encounters

THE CURRICULUM AND TESTING CONTEXT IN NEW YORK STATE

Over the last decade, the New York State Education Department has instituted curriculum and assessment policy changes under the mantle of raising educational standards. For middle and high school social studies teachers, these changes have taken form in new U.S. and global history and geography curricula and in new state exams at grades 8, 10, and 11.

The key curriculum documents are the *Learning Standards for Social Studies* (New York State Education Department, 1996) and the *Social Studies Resource Guide with Core Curriculum* (New York State Education Department, 1999). The *Learning Standards* describe the five overall content goals of the state social studies program. Those goals highlight the history of the United States and New York State, world history, geography, economics, and civics, citizenship, and government. Each of the standards is expressed in similar fashion. The first is illustrative: "Students will use a variety of intellectual skills to demonstrate their understanding of the major ideas, eras, themes, developments, and turning points in the history of the United States and New York." Each standard is divided into two or more *Key Ideas* which are further broken down into *Performance Indicators* for elementary, intermediate, and commencement levels.

The global nature of the *Learning Standards* is made more concrete in the *Core Curriculum*. In that document, a specific curriculum is presented for each school year. In outline fashion, the content ideas are keyed to the appropriate learning standard and a theme/concept. For example, the content idea "Constitutional Convention: Setting and Composition" reflects Learning Standard #5 and the concept of political systems. Essential questions and classroom connections are offered for each set of key content ideas.

Aside from coding the content ideas to the Learning Standards, relatively little is different in the latest version of the U.S. history and geography curriculum at grades 7–8 and 11 from previous incarnations. The bigger changes occurred in the new grades 9–10 global history and geography curriculum. There, the regional and cultural emphasis evident in the 1980s state curriculum was replaced with a chronological approach. The curriculum now features eight units, seven of which highlight a historical theme set within a chronological period.[2] For example, unit three, Global Interactions (1200–1650), includes attention to early Japanese history, the Mongols, global trade, the rise and fall of African civilizations (e.g., Ghana, Mali, Axum), and the Renaissance, Reformation, and rise of nation-states in Europe. In both the U.S. and global curricula, however, the emphasis is on a fairly predictable list of people, places, and events (Grant, 2001).

Change is far more evident in the new state social studies exams.[3] Overall, the biggest change is that all of the new state exams, administered now at grades 5, 8, 10, and 11, follow essentially the same format: multiple-choice questions, constructed-response questions, and a document-based question (DBQ).[4] Most readers well understand the nature of multiple-choice questions, and the New York test developers break no new ground here. Fewer readers will have had experience with constructed responses or DBQs, so we offer a bit of explanation below.

Constructed-response questions have two components—a primary or secondary source document and a set of one to three short-answer questions about the document. For example, the documents on the June 2003 grade 8 exam included a table showing differences between Federalists and Democratic-Republicans, a map depicting U.S. expansion in 1803, a letter written to Franklin Roosevelt during the Depression, and an excerpt from FDR's Four Freedoms speech. Three questions, calling largely for literal interpretations of the texts, followed each piece of text.[5]

Modeled after the document-based question on Advanced Placement (AP) history exams, the DBQs on the New York exams present students with six to eight primary and/or secondary texts (e.g., diary entries, portions of public speeches, political cartoons, graphs, textbook passages). The first charge is to read these texts and respond to one or two short-answer questions per document (as in the constructed-response section, most questions call only for literal interpretations). The students' second task is to respond to an essay prompt by drawing from the texts provided and from their outside knowledge. For example, the June 2003 grade 8 DBQ asked students to read and respond to texts about the Erie Canal and Transcontinental Railroad and to address this prompt: Discuss how the Erie Canal and Transcontinental Railroad led to economic growth in the United States.[6]

At grades 5 and 8, students' constructed-response answers are worth one point each, and their scores on this section are added to their scores on the multiple-choice section and the short-answer portion of the DBQ. The essay portion of the DBQ task is graded on a 0–5 point rubric. Those scores are added to the score from the constructed-response, multiple-choice, and short-answer questions to produce the final raw score.[7] Raw scores are then converted into a 1–4 scale grade. A raw score of 65–84 is assigned a grade of 3; a raw score of 85–100 is assigned a 4. Grades of 3 and 4 represent proficiency; scores of 1 or 2 represent substandard performance. For high school students, the raw scores are calculated in similar fashion (although with additional points from the thematic essay), but those scores are also the students' final scores. Thus, 65 represents a passing mark; 85 represents mastery level.

AMBITIOUS HISTORY TEACHING

Although there has been considerable research on the individual factors that influence teachers' practices (e.g., teachers' subject matter knowledge, teachers' expectations of students, and the contexts in which teachers work), relatively few researchers have tried to put multiple factors into play at the same time. Lee Shulman (1987) has done the field a huge service by looking at the intersection of two factors—teachers' knowledge of subject matter and knowledge of their students. His *pedagogical content knowledge* construct demonstrates the dynamic quality that defines a good portion of teachers' work. But teachers do not work in a vacuum. Moreover, the typical constraints teachers face (e.g., time, access to materials) are now joined by a new concern—the rise of high-stakes testing.

This emphasis on the multiple and interacting influences on teachers' work (Cornbleth, 2002; Grant, 2003; Romanowski, 1996; Sturtevant, 1996) suggests that separating teachers and their practices from the contexts in which they work offers little yield. The conditions that teachers face vary from one setting to the next, but all teachers face challenges of one sort or another.

Expressing the complexity of teachers' worlds, the construct of ambitious teaching presumes that teachers face many conditions—subject matter, students, state policies, colleagues, and administrators—which may confound their practices. Ambitious teachers take seriously those conditions, but in contrast to their less ambitious peers, they carve out pedagogical paths that aim toward more powerful teaching and learning. Ambitious teaching, then, is defined neither by innovations nor best practices alone. Ambitious teachers use newer teaching methods, alternative assessments, and flexible student groupings, but the mere evidence of these practices without the requisite signs of robust learning opportunities is insufficient to demonstrate ambitious teaching.

Of course, other factors likely matter too. Teacher beliefs and biography, students' socioeconomic class and family educational backgrounds, persistent patterns of race and class biases—these factors and more may influence the kinds of teaching and learning that develop in classrooms (Anyon, 1981; Dilworth, 2004; Eisenhart, Shrum, Harding, & Cuthbert, 1988; Grant, 1996; Pajares, 1992). We embrace the explanatory power of these considerations, but any examination of teachers' practices that puts every possible factor into play can result in analytic mush. So we take the approach that the three central features of ambitious teaching—knowledge of subject matter, knowledge of learners, and knowledge of context—give broad cover for the many other factors that influence teachers' pedagogical decisions and actions.

The literature base on ambitious teaching, while nowhere near comprehensive, is growing as researchers use the elements of this construct as a way of understanding the practices of the teachers they study (Gerwin & Visone, 2006; Gradwell, 2006; Grant, 2005; van Hover, 2006; Wineburg & Wilson, 1991; Yeager & Pinder, 2006).

The seeds for the ambitious teaching framework first were sown in Grant's (2003) study of two New York State high school teachers teaching about the U.S. civil rights movement. In this work, Grant discusses the interplay of forces at work when two teachers, sharing many similarities, construct learning environments fundamentally different from one another. He develops his ambitious teaching framework in more detail in a chapter in which he describes the journey a New York State global history and geography teacher takes as she navigates the recent changes in the state standards, curriculum, and tests (Grant, 2005). The teacher continually juggles the practical management of covering the vast grade 9–10 curriculum with her beliefs about good teaching. She allows neither the curriculum nor the test to dominate what she believes makes most sense for her students with regards to relevancy or engagement. And though the teacher is not always satisfied with her choices or the outcomes, her reflection and drive to make the next lesson better define her as ambitious. In short, ambitious teaching is an ongoing journey rather than a particular endpoint.

Gerwin and Visone (2006) investigated two secondary social studies teachers' aims, methods, materials, and classroom discussions in two of the courses each taught: one state-tested, the other an untested elective course with no state curriculum. In the courses that had state exams, the teachers focused on coverage of content through rote memorization; in the elective classes, they utilized more ambitious history teaching activities. The two teachers possessed the disciplinary knowledge and skills to foster ambitious learning environments yet chose to do so discriminately.

Like Grant (2003, 2005) and Gerwin and Visone (2006), Gradwell (2006) investigated a teacher from New York. Sarah Cooper, a third-year middle school teacher, taught five heterogeneously grouped sections of grade 8 U.S. history and prepared the students for the end of the year state exam. Unlike her peers in the school district, she focused less on test preparation strategies and more on exposing her students to a vast array of primary source documents and engaging them in authentic tasks and assessments. During a unit on the 1920s, Cooper devoted considerable time to exploring women's lives, though that topic is neither a focus in the state curriculum nor on past state tests. Cooper emerges as a case of teaching in spite of, rather than because of, the test.

In a study of seven beginning high school history teachers' perceptions of the Virginia state standards and tests, van Hover (2006) discovered that, although all had the potential for ambitious teaching, like most novice teachers, they concentrated on issues related to student management, learning the content, and managing a teaching schedule. As these teachers juggled daily classroom demands and a learning-on-the-job mentality, they did not resort to lecture or drill-and-kill teaching but instead used a variety of teaching techniques and assessments.

Yeager and Pinder (2006) looked at teachers' practices as they responded to the high-stakes testing climate in Florida. The two history teachers in their study, one a beginning white female teacher and the other a Hispanic female with seven years of full-time classroom experience, felt the weight of the state exam as they prepared lessons and implemented them in the classroom. Ironically, however, the Florida Comprehensive Assessment Test (FCAT) does not include any social studies content. It is the literacy portion of the test, then, that provides the context. Also, ironically, it is the veteran teacher who makes more accommodations to the state exam than her novice colleague. Both teachers, however, address the needs of their students, encourage them in the classroom, and engage them in rich historical content, all in less than the best circumstances.

TEACHING HISTORY WITH BIG IDEAS

Although the research base on ambitious teaching is growing, the empirical literature on teaching with big ideas largely begins with the teacher cases represented in this collection. A few authors (Gerwin & Visone, 2006; Kelly & VanSledright, 2005; Onosko & Swenson, 1996; Smith & Girod, 2003) describe elements of big idea teaching, but to this point, only two article-length studies detail the promise and problems of using big ideas to frame teachers' history instruction (Libresco, 2005; Wineburg & Wilson, 1991).

Some studies (e.g., Gerwin & Visone, 2006; Kelly & VanSledright, 2005) brush the surface of big idea teaching. For example, Gerwin and Visone mention briefly a secondary teacher's use of big ideas to frame the discussions in his elective U.S. history course. Sam Tookfield, one of the teachers in the study, included big ideas such as the following: "Were the 1950s a simpler time than today?" "Compare the Cuban missile crisis to the decision to invade Iraq." "Should the civil rights movement have ended when it did?" "Would you have been a successful sit-in participant?" and "Why do we have Black History Month? Should we?" No description of how these big ideas were created or how they were implemented in the classroom is provided, just a report that he used them.

Slightly more attention to the development and implementation of big ideas surfaces in Kelly and VanSledright's (2005) study. In the article, Kelly shares his early teaching experiences as he transformed from a collective-memory teacher to one who emphasized a more disciplinary-based approach. During his teaching internship, Kelly organized his content units around questions such as "Were all people in America included in the founders' vision?" and "Was a growing America a nation with a glorious destiny, or was it a vicious, hungry monster?" Kelly describes the struggles he endured as he attempted to use inquiry and interpretive exercises in his teaching.

Of the two full-length treatments of big idea teaching, the first is Wineburg and Wilson's (1991) comparative case study of two high school history teachers. To prepare for a debate about the legitimacy of British taxation in the American colonies, one of the teachers, Elizabeth Jensen, a grade 11 American history teacher, assigned numerous primary sources from the era and used big idea questions like "What are the sources of authority and freedom?" and "What are the costs and benefits of authority and freedom?" to foster her students' thinking about British-American relations of the time. The most powerful parts of Wineburg and Wilson's presentation are the words students offer as they engage with the ideas Jensen presents. The level of conversation—the questions (both factual and conceptual), ideas (concrete and abstract), and assertions that students made—demonstrates the power of teaching with big ideas.

In a another case study, Libresco (2005) investigated Paula Maron, a veteran grade 4 teacher, and her response to the implementation of the new New York State elementary social studies exam. Maron designed her curriculum around overarching questions. Her big idea question for the entire school year was "Has the history of New York State been a history of progress for all?" Additionally, Maron constructed a series of related big ideas for each of her units. For example, she asked her students "Did colonization of New York State result in progress for all?" "Did the American Revolution and Constitution result in progress for all?" "Did the modernization of New York State result in progress for all?" To assist her students in answering these broad questions, Maron provided primary sources, Internet sites, historical fiction, and other reference materials. Students worked individually and in small groups on various types of assessments such as essays, panel displays, human timelines, and role-plays. Libresco found that when Maron used big ideas to frame her units, she acted as a facilitator and was able to have students work as historians; engage in perspective-taking and historical empathy; learn reading, note-taking, communication, and focusing skills; and make connections across subject areas.

This smattering of research studies whets the appetite. Their findings demonstrate the power of good ideas to transform teachers' and students' classroom experiences. Missing, however, are deep explorations of the ideas, experiences, and outcomes of big idea teaching. No pedagogical approach comes without problems, and the teachers who report on their practices in this book record a range of challenges as they crafted their instructional approaches. But each teacher-author also records the energy and insights that developed as their students grappled with real ideas.

ORGANIZATION OF THE BOOK

Following this introductory chapter are the teacher-written case studies of big idea history teaching. The book then concludes with a chapter that provides a cross-case analysis, highlighting the patterns that emerge across the teacher-authors' reports, and a chapter that discusses the implications of the case studies, providing a road map for others' ambitious teaching in the future.

In chapter 2, Michael Meyer, a high school teacher in Clarence, New York, describes the three-year journey he took in building a big idea unit around the question "Why don't we know anything about Africa?" in his wealthy, suburban grade 10 global history and geography class. Meyer keys in on his own development as a teacher committed to ambitious teaching, but one who is initially unsure how to do it.

Working in an urban charter school, Megan Sampson, in chapter 3, tells a heartbreaking story of how the school context can upset even the most ambitious of teaching plans. Sampson details her experience in a global history and geography test preparation class. Her case features her description of how she used big ideas to teach a remedial class of urban students in preparation for the grade 10 state exam. Sampson's chapter highlights the critical role administrators can play in supporting or undermining a teacher's best efforts.

In chapter 4, Joseph Karb and Andrew Beiter, grade 8 history teachers in a rural middle school, make the case for using big ideas as a vehicle for bringing key historical events—both past and present— into their students' lives. They describe their approach to teaching the Nazi Holocaust in rich and dynamic ways, but they do so, in part, as a means of introducing the larger issue of genocide in human history.

In chapter 5, successful suburban teacher Tricia Davis describes her evolution as a teacher as she assumes a new position in an urban charter high school. With the use of big ideas in the background, Davis forefronts the challenges of teaching her students to learn historical content through a new approach to writing, one that pays off in terms of increasing students' historical knowledge and under-standing as well as their state test scores.

Suburban middle school teacher Sarah Foels discusses in chapter 6 the benefits of developing and using big ideas for a diverse set of learners in social studies. Experimenting with both honors and inclusion classrooms at the middle school level, she discovers that all students are capable of relating to and thinking deeply about content through the use of big ideas. Although the challenges of standardized testing and differentiated learning initially make her hesitant to try out big ideas in her transition from teaching an honors class to teaching an inclusion class, Foels recognizes the importance of showing every student how to form her or his own answers to the key questions in the curriculum.

Julie Doyle, a rural grade 10 teacher, traces in chapter 7 her implementation of a unit on nineteenth-century European imperialism around the big idea "Does imperialism help or hurt native peoples?" Doyle discovers that when she teaches with big ideas, coupled with the use of teacher and student blogs, her students make strong connections to the past, acquire confidence in their argumentative skills, and overall seem more engaged in the learning of history.

In chapter 8, grade 11 suburban teacher Mary Beth Bruce demonstrates how big idea teaching can work in an Advanced Placement U.S. history course. Bruce first argues that even content-heavy courses like AP U.S. history can be organized around big idea questions. Second, she demonstrates in convincing fashion how students can develop their own big ideas.

In chapter 9, our cross-case analysis, we describe and analyze the patterns of possibilities and problems that surface in the teachers' presentations. The possibilities include richer and more complex subject matter taught, more varied teaching and assessment approaches, and more consideration of the interests and abilities that all students bring to class. The problems include finding the right classroom assessments, facing administrative realities, and coming to terms with the evolutionary nature of one's teaching practice. We argue, as the teachers do, that the potential for big idea teaching clearly outweighs the associated problems.

Any book that features rich, in-depth portraits of teachers at work is likely to have implications for other teachers and students. But in chapter 10, we note implications for two other groups as well—teacher educators and academic researchers. The former are likely to see both the challenges and opportunities available as they work to raise the expectations of their prospective and practicing teacher-students. The latter are likely to view the teacher cases as part of the emerging research literature on ambitious teaching, a literature that deserves further investigation and elaboration.

CONCLUSION

Ambitious teaching is no nirvana, a state that one achieves and then never leaves. Using big ideas to frame one's practice allows for richer and more complex subject matter, more varied teaching and assessment approaches, and more consideration of the interests and abilities that all students bring to class. At the same time, ambitious teachers must navigate a rocky road, one that includes the need to seize control of the curriculum, come to terms with the evolutionary nature of one's teaching practice, and respond to administrative realities. These issues present no small set of obstacles. But we assert, as the teachers do, the potential for ambitious teaching clearly outweighs the associated problems.

NOTES

1. In this chapter, we use the terms "social studies" and "history" interchangeably.

2. The eighth unit, Global Connection and Interactions, focuses on a range of issues: migration, technology, status of women and children, ethnic and religious tensions.

3. A description of the new exams and sample questions are available at the New York State social studies Web site: www.emsc.nysed.gov/ciai/social.html.

4. The grade 10 and 11 tests also include a thematic essay.

5. The third question under each document asked students to recall a piece of information not apparent in the document and presumably learned during class.

6. In addition to the constructed-response and DBQ tasks, students answer forty-five multiple-choice questions.

7. Adding the multiple-choice, constructed-response, and short-answer questions together, students can earn up to 69 points. Point totals are calibrated, however, such that 59 points earns a passing score of 65. That means students can pass the exam without even writing the DBQ essay.

REFERENCES

Anderson, G. L., & Herr, K. (1999). The new paradigm wars: Is there room for rigorous practitioner knowledge in schools and universities? *Educational Researcher, 28*(5), 12–21.

Anyon, J. (1981). Social class and school knowledge. *Curriculum Inquiry, 11*(1), 3–42.

Cochran-Smith, M., & Lytle, S. (1993). *Inside/outside: Teacher research and knowledge.* New York: Teachers College Press.

Cornbleth, C. (2002). What constrains meaningful social studies teaching. *Social Education, 63*(3), 186–190.

Cusick, P. A. (1983). *The egalitarian ideal and the American high school.* New York: Longman.

Dewey, J. (1902/1969). *The child and the curriculum.* Chicago: University of Chicago Press.

Dilworth, P. (2004). Multicultural citizenship education: Case studies from social studies classrooms. *Theory and Research in Social Education, 32*(2), 53–186.

Eisenhart, M., Shrum, J., Harding, J., & Cuthbert, A. (1988). Teacher beliefs: Definitions, findings, and directions. *Educational Policy, 2,* 51–70.

Epstein, T. (1994). *America Revised* revisited: Adolescents' attitudes towards a United States history textbook. *Social Education, 58*(1), 41–44.

Evans, R. (2004). *The social studies wars: What should we be teaching the children?* New York: Teachers College Press.

Gerwin, D., & Visone, F. (2006). The freedom to teach: Contrasting history teaching in elective and state-tested courses. *Theory and Research in Social Education, 34*(2), 259–282.

Goodlad, J. (1984). *A place called school.* New York: McGraw-Hill.

Gradwell, J. M. (2006). Teaching in spite of, rather than because of, the test: A case of ambitious history teaching in New York State. In S. G. Grant (Ed.), *Measuring history: Cases of high-stakes testing across the U.S.* (pp. 157–176). Greenwich, CT: Information Age.

Grant, S. G. (1996). Locating authority over content and pedagogy: Cross-current influences on teachers' thinking and practice. *Theory and Research in Social Education, 24*(3), 237–272.

——. (2001). When an "A" isn't enough: Analyzing the New York State global history exam. *Educational Policy Analysis Archives, 9*(39).

——. (2003). *History lessons: Teaching, learning, and testing in U.S. high school classrooms.* Mahwah, NJ: Lawrence Erlbaum.

——. (2005). More journey than end: A case of ambitious teaching. In E. A. Yeager & O. L. Davis Jr. (Eds.), *Wise social studies teaching in an age of high-stakes testing* (pp. 117–130). Greenwich, CT: Information Age.

Grant, S. G., & VanSledright, B. (2006). *Elementary social studies: Constructing a powerful approach to teaching and learning* (2nd ed.). Boston, MA: Houghton Mifflin.

Hawkins, D. (1974). I, thou, and it. *The informed vision: Essays on learning and human nature* (pp. 48–62). New York: Agathon.

Kelly, T., & VanSledright, B. (2005). A journey toward wiser practice in the teaching of American history. In E. Yeager & O. L. Davis (Eds.), *Wise social studies teaching in an age of high-stakes testing* (pp. 183–202). Greenwich, CT: Information Age.

Lapp, M., Grigg, W., & Tay-Lim, B. (2002). *The nation's report card: U.S. history 2001.* Washington, DC: U.S. Department of Education, National Center for Education Statistics.

Levstik, L. (2008). What happens in social studies classrooms? In L. Levstik & C. Tyson (Eds.), *Handbook of research in social studies education* (pp. 50–62). New York: Routledge.

Libresco, A. (2005). How she stopped worrying and learned to love the test . . . sort of. In E. Yeager & O. L. Davis Jr. (Eds.), *Wise social studies teaching in an age of high-stakes testing* (pp. 33–49). Greenwich, CT: Information Age.

Nash, G., Crabtree, C., & Dunn, R. (2000). *History on trial: Culture wars and the teaching of the past.* New York: Vintage.

New York State Education Department. (1996). *Learning standards for social studies.* Albany, NY: Author.

——. (1999). *Social studies resource guide with core curriculum.* Albany, NY: Author.

Onosko, J., & Swenson, L. (1996). Designing issue-based unit plans. In R. Evans & D. Saxe (Eds.), *Handbook on teaching social issues* (pp. 89–98). Washington, DC: National Council for the Social Studies.

Pajares, M. (1992). Teachers' beliefs and educational research: Cleaning up a messy construct. *Review of Educational Research, 62*, 307–332.

Romanowski, M. (1996). Issues and influences that shape the teaching of U.S. history. In J. Brophy (Ed.), *Advances in research on teaching: Vol. 6* (pp. 291–312). Greenwich, CT: JAI.

Schug, M., Todd, R., & Beery, R. (1984). Why kids don't like social studies. *Social Education, 47*(5), 382–387.

Schwab, J. (1978). The practical: Translation into curriculum. In I. Westbury & I. Wilkof (Eds.), *Science, curriculum, and liberal education* (pp. 365–383). Chicago: University of Chicago Press.

Shulman, L. (1987). Knowledge and teaching: Foundations of the new reform. *Harvard Educational Review, 57*(1), 1–22.

Smith, J., & Girod, M. (2003). John Dewey and psychologizing the subject matter: Big ideas, ambitious teaching, and teacher education. *Teaching and Teacher Education, 19*(3), 295–307.

Sturtevant, E. (1996). Lifetime influences on the literacy-related instructional beliefs of experienced high school history teachers: Two comparative case studies. *Journal of Literacy Research, 28*(2), 227–257.

Thornton, S. (2004). *Teaching social studies that matters: Curriculum for active learning.* New York: Teachers College Press.

——. (2008). Continuity and change in social studies curriculum. In L. Levstik & C. Tyson (Eds.), *Handbook of research in social studies classrooms* (pp. 15–32). New York: Routledge.

van Hover, S. (2006). Teaching history in the Old Dominion: The impact of Virginia's accountability reform on seven secondary beginning history teachers. In S. G. Grant (Ed.), *Measuring history: Cases of high-stakes testing across the U.S.* (pp. 195–220). Greenwich, CT: Information Age.

Wineburg, S., & Wilson, S. (1991). Subject matter knowledge in the teaching of history. In J. Brophy (Ed.), *Advances in research on teaching* (pp. 305–347). Greenwich, CT: JAI.

Yeager, E., & Pinder, M. (2006). "Does anyone really understand this test?" Florida high school social studies teachers' efforts to make sense of the FCAT. In S. G. Grant (Ed.), *Measuring history: Cases of state-level reform across the United States* (pp. 249–272). Greenwich, CT: Information Age.

2

THE EVOLUTION OF A BIG IDEA: WHY DON'T WE KNOW ANYTHING ABOUT AFRICA?

Michael Meyer

I didn't start out as a teacher. After college, I pursued a career in business for about seven years. While financially rewarding, business was unsatisfying, so I looked for a career that had rewards beyond money alone. I come from a family of teachers and I decided that maybe my calling was in the field. The whole point of my change in careers was to seek something more than money.

When I thought about teaching, I was hoping to do a couple of things. The first was to help my students become skeptical consumers of information: to question what they hear and are told and to seek answers for themselves. In a world of limitless information and ubiquitous media, critical or skeptical thinking is an important skill to teach if we are to create responsible citizens. The second thing was to help students become more tolerant and to realize that there is a diverse and interesting world around them filled with all kinds of people. I was hoping to encourage students to accept and embrace the differences among people. In an increasingly global world, it is important for students to be better world citizens.

Of course, these goals are easier said than done. And when I started teaching, I looked at the goals I had and what I was doing and they didn't seem to match. Especially in my first year, I felt trapped in the curriculum and nervous about the test my students would take at the end of their sophomore year. I guess on some level I hoped that if I could just get through the stuff for my course this year and finish graduate school, then I would be able to teach the way I wanted to teach "later."

I think that my experience as a first- and second-year teacher was pretty typical. I was teaching courses for the first time, trying to finish my master's degree, coaching, paying a mortgage, and helping to raise my children, all while trying to teach kids and get tenured. Needless to say, I felt the pinch.

In graduate school, I was exposed to a number of theories on how to be a better teacher and how to make powerful learning happen for students. I read Wiggins and McTighe (1998), Grant (2003), and Barton and Levstik (2004). I learned about big ideas, inquiry-based learning, differentiated instruction, and teaching for participatory democracy. The subtext of all of these courses and all of these texts was that teachers were not doing these things, that students were worse off because of it, and that truly exceptional teachers who cared about their students would invest the time to teach in these new and improved ways.

But what about me? I wanted to be an exceptional teacher. I cared. I worked hard. Yet I wasn't doing this stuff: I wasn't teaching with big ideas, I wasn't differentiating instruction, and I wasn't teaching students to be prepared to be citizens in our participatory democracy. In short, I really wasn't meeting the goals that I had set for myself as a teacher. What more could I do? How did people find the time to do all this stuff? Were the "exceptional teachers" people with no lives who spent their mornings and evenings looking for primary sources, coming up with great plans, and knowing the personal details and learning needs of every single kid?

My answer to all of these questions was simple. Yes this stuff sounds great, and I *will* do it. Just not now.

What follows is a description of how I came to see that ambitious teaching, specifically teaching with big ideas, really is doable as long as you look at it as a continual process. The answer to my question of when I would have time to come up with this stuff is that I didn't need to come up with it all at once. This chapter looks at the evolution of a unit that I teach about Africa. It describes how one unit and one simple idea can provide a path to teaching with big ideas.

SCHOOL BACKGROUND AND TEACHING TO THE TEST

I teach in one of the most affluent and successful school districts in western New York State. The high school and the school district generally are consistently ranked in the top three in area rankings. The school has also received the Blue Ribbon National School of Excellence distinction. My school offers twenty Advanced Placement classes, the school average on SATs is 1100, and 90 percent of the students go on to post-secondary education.

In other words, my school is a great place to teach. The students generally come from families where education is valued, the community is supportive of a wide variety of school activities, and the administration provides a climate that is safe and dedicated to high standards. However, these high standards come with clear pressure from the community and school board on the administration, teachers, and students of the district to maintain our top ranking.

As for the pressure placed on teachers to get the students to do well on their state tests, the story of my new teacher orientation should suffice. At this meeting, the principal announced his position with regard to the Regents tests: "Just so there is no confusion about whether or not you should be teaching to the tests, let me be clear: teach to the test—it is how you will be evaluated."

At this point, it may seem like I am whining with regard to the pressure that we face in my school district. But different schools present different challenges to teachers. I am aware that in many school districts, the main concern is just to get students to *pass* the tests. In our school and community, it is *assumed* that we will get all the kids to pass the tests, that is, to achieve a score of 65 or above. So for us, the goal is to get as many students as possible to achieve a score of 85 or above. The mark of 85 and above is considered mastery level in New York and is especially coveted because, across the state and especially in our area, school rankings seem to be an obsession of administrators, board members, and taxpayers, not to mention the media. And what generally differentiates the top schools is students' performance at the mastery level. So the pressure isn't for achieving passing scores; it is for excelling.

To this end, it is made clear to us from the beginning that tenure decisions are made almost exclusively on the 85 or above criterion. Every year, we begin with a meeting with the principal where he repeatedly cites this number as a goal. And during every in-service day, the 85 or above goal is listed as one of the objectives. Most, if not all, of the untenured teachers in my school fear the state tests and obsess over content. My sense is that the vast majority of decisions made by teachers in their first few years involve covering curriculum rather than teaching meaningful lessons.

Yet the pressure continues even once one has earned tenure. In a meeting about a new push in our school to get more kids to the 85 or above benchmark, a colleague of mine who has been teaching over fifteen years said, "I used to spend way more time on class projects and discussion lessons but now feel like I have to constantly push content just to get it all in." Further, he said that because of the additional pressure being placed on teachers with regard to 85 or above, "this is the first year where teaching has felt like a job."

Basically, the culture here is to teach to the test, and most if not all teachers comply. Although many studies that we read in graduate school say that if one teaches with big ideas and in other ambitious ways, student achievement will improve, most teachers do not think there is enough time to teach in these innovative ways and cover everything that needs to be covered. Teachers can teach however they want, but the pressure here is toward coverage and away from more ambitious ways of teaching.

MY INTRODUCTION TO TEACHING ABOUT AFRICA

My first year at Clarence High, I taught senior-year government and economics courses which, although state-mandated, have no state tests associated with them. In many ways, these were like teaching elective courses. Since there were no test results at the end of the year on which I would be evaluated, I felt that there was time to explore fewer topics and in greater depth. Also I felt more comfortable experimenting with innovative lessons and units without having to worry so much about coverage.

The next year, I taught grade 9 global history and geography for the first time. In addition to taking on a new preparation, I was in the middle of coaching my first season of volleyball, had a one-year-old at home, and was taking a master's level class. I was still untenured and felt strongly that I was to be evaluated heavily on my students' achievement on our common assessment.[1] In other words, I felt as though I didn't have enough time to think about the best ways to teach everything that I was supposed to teach. I was in survival mode.

When I reached the point in the curriculum where I was to teach about early Africa, I felt at a loss. In fact, other than the slave trade, I really didn't know where to start. I was a U.S. history major in college and really had not thought much about Africa since maybe my own grade 9 class. Without much content background of my own, I searched for help. I first looked at the New York State curriculum and saw very little in there about Africa. In a curriculum of forty single-spaced pages, ancient African civilizations[2] were reduced to a list:

Rise and fall of African civilizations: Ghana, Mali, Axum, and Songhai empires

1. Human and physical geography
2. Organization structure
3. Contributions
4. Roles in global trade routes

5. Spread and impact of Islam—Mansa Musa
6. Timbuktu and African trade routes

Finding this list not very instructive, I went through some past New York State Regents global history exams. This exam is given three times a year, and all the teachers in New York know, in spite of what the curriculum writers might say, that the questions on the exams have a way of repeating themselves. Aware of this tendency, I thought that the exams would be a good place to start to make sure that I at least covered the information on which the students would be tested. Past exams, however, were not particularly helpful.

Basically, I saw three questions. One was about the gold-salt trade, one was about the Bantu migrations, and one was about how there had been civilizations in Africa before the Europeans arrived. I found it interesting that the state asked a question pointing out there were civilizations before the Europeans arrived but did not ask about those civilizations. I also thought it was unfortunate that the area of the world about which my students probably knew the least required me to teach the least about it. I started to feel that it was wrong to send the message to the students that Africa doesn't matter.

When I talked to some teachers about what the kids really needed to know about Africa, the first answer I got was "Nothing." As I pressed further, I got "Teach something about the Bantu migrations . . . they ask that every year." Then I got what turned out to be a similar response from two other teachers, one of whom said, "Let me put it this way, I am teaching and testing about Africa on Friday." This attitude was confirmed later in the year when I was walking through one of the teacher's classrooms. As he was putting up his overhead of notes about Africa, he said, "I have to apologize about this unit . . . it is a bit like a Hoover vacuum . . . it sucks."

The bottom line is that most of my colleagues viewed Africa as something to be covered for the test. Africa was a few bullet points to be tested with three questions. So why spend more than a day on Africa?

Finally, I talked to another teacher with whom I share a similar philosophy of teaching. He told me that he starts off his unit on Africa by asking the question "Why don't we know anything about Africa?" Little did I know that this simple question was going to be the beginning of my understanding of what it meant to teach big ideas. The truth is that, although it may seem I was taking an ambitious route to teaching, I was actually still in survival mode and looking for the easiest route. This teacher had a good idea of what to teach and the materials to go along with it. I happened upon teaching with big ideas because, in this case at least, it appeared to be easier. By that I mean, rather than coming up with my own unit, I had the beginnings of an ambitious big idea unit handed to me.

THE EVOLUTION OF THE UNIT

After my colleague asked the question, my response was "I don't know . . . why don't we?" From that point, we discussed how little is required of students throughout high school and beyond and why that is. He brought up issues of slavery, imperialism, and continuing problems of race. I began to see how the fact that we know so little about Africa reveals much about history and our modern views on the world. My friend's simple question stayed with me as I tried to plan a unit on Africa. In doing so, I discovered two things. The first was that I didn't know anything about Africa. The second was that this unit, for me, wasn't just about Africa anymore.

First Steps toward a Big Idea Unit

The first year I started the discussion of Africa with the simple question of why we don't know anything about Africa, students responded with comments like "Because there is nothing there," "Because nobody ever taught us about it," and "Because nothing good ever came out of Africa." I asked follow-up questions that, I think, revealed much of what I wanted them to learn on their own. Rather than simply asking "Why do you think that is?" or "What proof do you have of that?" I asked questions like "Does it tell you anything about how we value Africa by what we don't know?" and "What does that tell you about how we view Africans today?"

The unit then featured a series of teacher-created PowerPoint presentations, a movie, and a Regents-style test. For extra credit, I asked the students to explain why Africa matters. What they wrote sounded very similar to all the points I had made the first day. They wrote things like "Because learning about Africa's history might affect how we view Africa today" and "Maybe if people knew that Africa had a history it could help with racism." Although I was thrilled to read these things, I realized that I was hearing my own voice way too clearly to show any sort of meaningful learning. Students were repeating what they thought I wanted to hear rather than writing something meaningful that they had learned on their own. Basically, the mistake I made my first year was in *teaching* too much rather than letting the students reach their own conclusions.

As the Africa unit approached during my second year of teaching global history, I was keen to improve the unit and to help my students see how things like history and race have been constructed throughout time. I started with a KWL chart[3] to make explicit their knowledge and feelings toward the subject. I thought that it was important for the students to see how little they knew about Africa and to see the underlying prejudices that they had toward Africa past and present. As I suspected, the kids had little or no knowledge of Africa, and what they did know centered on things like slavery, war, and disease. Further, they believed the reason for their lack of knowledge was that there was/is nothing of value in Africa. Actual responses of students about what they knew about Africa included comments such as "Don't people all live in huts there?" "Aren't there a lot of wars?" and "Nothing."

With these responses, I felt that there was an opportunity to teach the kids a lesson about more than ancient African civilizations. Unfortunately, I once again interjected too much of what I wanted the kids to learn by the end of the first discussion. Rather than let the students discover knowledge and have personal "aha" moments, I basically beat them over the head with my own beliefs from the beginning: the case of Africa shows where race and power can affect history and how that flawed history can continue to affect modern views of race and power; history and racism are historically connected and constructed; to address modern problems, it can be instructive to examine where they came from. Although I think that many of the kids got the point of what I was trying to teach them, a lot of them tuned out as they figured out what they thought I wanted them to know.

Reflections and Changes

Reflecting on how the unit had gone the first two years, I realized that *I* was the problem. Rather than letting the discussion develop from the student perspective, I ended up asking many leading questions. After I asked the question "Why don't we know anything about Africa?" many students responded that they hadn't been taught anything about Africa. I immediately pounced on this and asked, "Why is that?" They responded with a lot of the kinds of guesses described above. Rather than writing these ideas down and using them as points of departure, I immediately started refuting their ideas and telling them information from the unit. Finally, I ended up asking a lot of "Don't you think . . . ?" questions that obviously revealed my beliefs.

Since I was taking the time to try to teach the students something meaningful, I didn't want them to tell me only what they thought I wanted them to think about Africa. I wanted them to actually *think* about Africa and create meaning from the ideas for themselves. I wasn't trying to cover content for a test; I was trying to get them to think about a larger set of issues.

I think I taught the way I did for those first couple of years because I wasn't really sure of what I wanted them to get out of it and I wasn't always sure where the discussion would go if I let it have a life of its own. The real result was that when we came to later discussions and also their final assessments, I could hear my voice in their voices and writing. Maybe some students got the point, but I think that most were telling me what they thought I wanted to hear. Many students echoed the exact words that I gave them in response to my first-day question of "Why does Africa matter?" They wrote things like "Because how we view Africa in the past affects how we view Africa, Africans, and African Americans today" and "If we can understand how racism affects history, maybe we can think about how it continues to affect society today." These were great responses, but they sounded far too much like things I had said earlier in the unit. So I took these responses less as evidence of learning and more as evidence of repeating information for a grade.

The third time I taught the global history course, I was very conscious not to interject so much of my own voice into the initial and later discussions. I asked similar initial questions, but I allowed students to comment on each others' ideas. For example, the most common initial response to my question about why we don't know anything about Africa was "Because we haven't been taught anything about Africa." My response to this was "Well, why do you think that is?" In the past, I would have followed my initial open-ended question with others that would have tipped my hand about the "right" answers. I would have asked questions like "What does this tell you about how we value Africa?" or "Don't you think this teaches you that Africa isn't important?"

This time, I allowed students to explore their own reasoning. Some students guessed "Nothing happened there," "Nothing has been discovered," "They didn't write," "They didn't trade," and "They aren't important." This time, rather than my addressing these reasons directly, we wrote these ideas down in order to see how these hunches might later turn out. Using this list as a foil for the rest of the unit was very effective as students crossed their previous guesses from the list as they uncovered information about the African civilizations. For my part, I guided the discussions with very little comment, let the students research the information they needed, and allowed them the freedom to explore the difficult issues that were raised by this unit. Their conclusions—that there were great civilizations in Africa, that historians have known about them for years, and that there has been an intentional attempt made for 500 years to ignore that history—were completely their own. From these ideas came discussions about the legacy of slavery, imperialism in Africa, and racism at home.

The Unit as It Currently Stands

What follows is a series of snapshots of the lessons that currently make up my unit.

Day 1: Students complete the "know" and "want to know" sections of a KWL chart.

We do KWL activities from time to time in my class, and the students are familiar with them. I instruct students to only think of things that they know about Sub-Saharan Africa. Inevitably the students say they know nothing, or they offer only information about after the Europeans arrive (e.g., slavery) or modern negatives (e.g., war, disease). This activity leads into a discussion of "Why do you think we know so little about Africa?" Usually they start with things like "Because we haven't learned about it yet." I then remind them of how much they knew when they did KWLs on Greece, Rome, China, and Egypt and ask why they knew so much about these civilizations and so little about Africa. When they respond "Because we haven't been taught anything about Africa," I press them to try to figure out why *that* was. They then come up with things such as "Because there isn't anything there," "Nothing important happened there," and the like. I interject very little and just jot down their reasons.

We then complete the "W" (or "what I *want* to learn") part. Here, the students start to have general questions such as "Were there any empires there?" and "Did anything happen there?" I let these questions go for later discussion.

Day 2: Students read and discuss several primary source documents from travelers who went to various African empires before the age of imperialism.

The two readings that I have found work best are excerpts from *Periplus of the Erythrean Sea* and *The Book of Roger* by Al-Idrisi. The reason I find these texts most helpful is that, at this point of the year, we have learned about the golden ages of Greece and of the empires of Islam. Hearing me tell them that there was greatness in Africa is not nearly as convincing to them as hearing voices from two civilizations that they regard as advanced describing that greatness. It is a chance to see that travelers from the most advanced of civilizations of the time were impressed with what they encountered in Africa. Light bulbs start to go on as they see Greeks describe Africans as highly civilized and prosperous and Muslim traders describe the wealth of Africa. This is the first time they have learned that "there was something there."

I then show the students a PowerPoint on Kush and Axum, including images of the art and architecture of these kingdoms. Typically, they are amazed that such fabulous kingdoms existed before the arrival of Europeans.

Days 3–5: Students create PowerPoint presentations on one of the African empires.

Depending on the size of the group, I tend to let the students choose between Ghana, Mali, Songhai, Benin, Axum, and Zimbabwe. The students work in groups and have library and computer time. The emphasis is on finding images of and primary source writings about or from these empires. The guiding question for the students in all groups is "What was in Africa before the Europeans showed up?"

The student inquiries are mostly fact based. Students are tasked with finding out things such as where the empire was, how it came to power, who its important rulers were, what its main accomplishments were, why it lost power, and with whom it traded. The point here is to encourage them to see the art, architecture, and literature of civilizations that they previously had no idea existed. In the end, they are asked to list the three most important things they learned from creating their PowerPoint. Often the principal thing they say they learned is "There was actually something there."

Days 6–7: Students present and discuss their projects.

Students present PowerPoint presentations of approximately ten slides. All students in each group are expected to present, and one large part of the grading involves being able to explain more information than the bullet points on the slides. This usually takes the form of describing the pictures from the slides or the quotes from or about famous Africans. Typically each presentation lasts from ten to twenty minutes.

At the end, students are asked to answer the following question: "Which is the greatest empire and why?" I don't give them criteria to determine what it means to be a great civilization; I just pose the question. We then spend time discussing their answers and their criteria. Students seem to forget that "there isn't anything in Africa." The idea is that if they are debating which civilization is the greatest, then their thinking is well beyond "was there anything there?"

I am also interested to see what criteria the students use for defining what a great civilization is. I am hoping here to show them how culturally defined their criteria are. In other words, they tend to pick the civilizations with the biggest buildings and the most trade. By their own definitions, I hope to show them how their definitions would exclude many of the civilizations outside of Europe and Europe's sphere of influence.

Finally, I use the question about a greatest African civilization to set up the movie and thesis for the next two days by getting the kids into a whole new level of discussion about Africa.

Days 8–9: Students view Time-Life Lost Civilizations series movie, *Africa: A History Denied.* Completion of the L part of the KWL chart.

The thesis of this video is that there has been a deliberate attempt by Western and Muslim societies to deny Africa its history in order to accommodate their imperialist agendas. After the movie, we discuss again the question of why we know so little about African history. Usually we end up touching on modern preconceived notions, racism, and other important topics.

Then, students fill in the "L" (or "what I learned") part of the KWL chart. Responses vary from the general (e.g., "I learned that there was something in Africa") to the more specific and analytical (e.g., "I learned that because of things like imperialism and racism, Africa has been denied a history"). I also receive responses such as "Nothing" and "There were civilizations in Africa, but none of them were that great."

Day 10: Essay test.
The final assessment of this unit is an essay where students are asked to explain why they think it is important to learn about African history. We conclude by discussing their answers.

WHAT DO STUDENTS GET OUT OF THE BIG IDEA?

Although I can never be certain exactly what the kids have learned from the unit, I have taken their concluding answers to "Why don't we know anything about Africa?" and "Why does Africa matter?" as proof of some change. Whereas in the beginning of the unit they were inclined to say things like "There was nothing there" and "Africa doesn't matter," by the end these views typically have changed. Many students will say "Europeans have tried to hide the history" or "White people don't want to believe that Africans could have been so advanced." Finally, when a student writes something like "Learning about Africa is important because it might change how we view people of color today," I feel that I have achieved something. In past years, I may have found that students were merely repeating something they had heard me say earlier in the unit, but this year I felt as though these ideas were their own responses and showed evidence of learning.

I am sure that some of these responses sound much like the ones offered when I was sure that the students were just telling me things they had heard me say or things they thought that I wanted to hear. However, I am more confident that these are their own responses and that these responses demonstrate real learning because I am careful not to say any of the things that I hope they learn throughout the lesson. The biggest thing that I hope they get is a feeling of "Hey, it *is* weird that we don't know anything about Africa" and "There are very important reasons for it."

When we conclude our discussion of the big question of "Why don't we know anything about Africa?" we refer back to the list that we came up with at the beginning of the unit. We cross off things like "Because there was nothing there" and "Because historians don't know anything about it." Typically we end up crossing off all of the possibilities that we came up with. We are left then with the thesis from the movie, that there has been a deliberate attempt to deprive Africa of its history. The evidence for this assertion comes in the form of the knowledge we have uncovered about what we as historians actually do know about Africa. When I ask questions about their thinking here, they will say things like "Well, if we know all this stuff about Africa and don't teach it, it just seems obvious that people are trying to ignore it or hide it for some reason."

That said, I am sure that not all the students are getting it. In fact, I do admit that there are definitely those who don't or won't get it. One year, at least two students in response to the question "Why does Africa matter?" simply wrote "It doesn't."

One encouraging thing that I have witnessed is that often students who are not usually successful on traditional assessments become the ones who seem to take the lead in many of the discussions in this unit and often come up with the most compelling answers at the end. And while many of them continue to struggle with the traditional assessments that we must give in preparation for the mandated tests, I think that the experience of success in these types of units, as well as the larger lessons that they are hopefully learning, are meaningful to them.

WHAT I LEARNED ABOUT BIG IDEA TEACHING

I have learned a couple of things through this process and through reflecting on the process. The first is that my graduate school professors were correct. I found that when I taught with big ideas, when I allowed students to search for answers, and when I led a class without "leading" the class, students were more engaged, more willing to take on bigger concepts, and more able to look at issues bigger than information for a test. Hopefully this experience will help them to be more skeptical of and to look differently at the world around them. In other words, for those of us in teaching for more than test results, using big ideas can help us actually teach the kids something.

The second thing I learned is that there is time to implement these ideas. As I said above, I didn't plan on teaching this unit as a big idea unit. However, as time passed, I realized that I was teaching a big idea unit and that there was time to add, subtract, and improve what I was doing. Most of us in teaching will be doing this for thirty years or more. There may not be time to plan the best big idea unit about Africa for next week, but once I started on the path, I realized that I could teach some form of a big idea unit about Africa this year and plan for a better big idea unit next year. The point here is to start somewhere. Moreover, having seen the results of this type of teaching, I am exploring additional big idea units around the following: "What does it mean to be barbaric?" for a unit on the Mongols; "Are Native Americans civilized?" for a unit on exploration and encounter; and "Is the process for making laws in our country broken?" for a unit on Congress.

Moreover, my Africa unit is still not "finished." At this point, I am hoping to teach this unit in similar fashion in future years. However, there is still room for improvement. An ambitious way to take this unit a step further might be to start with the questions "What is racism?" and "Where does it come from?" My thought is to start off with these questions even before the students construct their answers to the KWL. I am not sure what will come of this one change, but I am interested to see the results. The point here is that modifying units like this is a never-ending process with many different possibilities.

Lastly, I have learned that implementing ideas from graduate school such as the big idea is a process. I know of no teacher who has implemented all of these ideas for all of his or her units. But what I do hear from like-minded colleagues is that they are struggling every year to improve on what they did the year before. With this unit, I jotted down notes from year to year so that when Africa was coming up, I could improve upon and expand what I did the year before. This idea that units evolve, that is, that my teaching evolves, is what I most learned from all of this process.

NOTES

1. The grade 9 common assessment is not a state exam but is one that my colleagues and I develop from past Regents questions.

2. There are later references in the curriculum to Africa. However, this list represents the only part of the curriculum that deals with Africa before the era of European imperialism.

3. A KWL chart is a graphic organizer on which students track what they know (K), what they want to know (W), and what they have learned (L). Students discuss and answer the first two sections as the unit begins and the third at the end.

REFERENCES

Barton, K., & Levstik, L. (2004). *Teaching history for the common good*. Mahwah, NJ: Lawrence Erlbaum.

Grant, S. G. (2003). *History lessons: Teaching, learning, and testing in U.S. high school classrooms*. Mahwah, NJ: Lawrence Erlbaum.

Wiggins, G., & McTighe, J. (1998). *Understanding by design*. Alexandria, VA: ASCD.

3

DEFINING SUCCESS WITH BIG IDEAS: A NEW TEACHER'S GROWTH AND CHALLENGES

Megan Sampson

Big ideas—everything in my first year of teaching seemed like a big idea. I had to find my voice, modify my goals, and navigate the politics and culture of my school environment. Fresh out of college and my education classes, I jumped into the classroom with all the drive and ambition a new teacher could have. I wanted to make a difference; I wanted to teach in a way that resonated with my students; I wanted to prepare my students to succeed in a world of standardized tests and high expectations. Big ideas, I thought, fit into my teaching goals; they would help me bring the intricacies of history into perspective for my students while at the same time giving them the skills and confidence to succeed on the state exam. When I learned about the concept of big ideas, I was excited to put them into practice. This approach allowed me to think beyond the core curriculum and state tests and develop questions that would anchor my unit and get my students thinking. Each question was designed to facilitate higher-level thinking while at the same time lending interest and enthusiasm to the topic. The concept of big ideas motivated me, and I wanted them to motivate my students as well.

I started my first year teaching four classes of Global History and Geography I (ancient world history to the Renaissance) and one class of Global History and Geography II (world history from the Age of Exploration to the present). In the second semester, I was given a new assignment. My task: to prepare a small group of students for the upcoming global history state exam in June—students who had been unsuccessful with this exam on multiple occasions. By this time, I had a semester of teaching under my belt and felt eager to take on this new challenge. I felt that this would be the perfect avenue to test my theories on big ideas; I could condense the curriculum, make it relevant to the students through the use of big ideas, and have tangible results to analyze in only a few months. I felt confident that I could help them succeed.

Despite my enthusiasm and confidence, the semester did not develop as I had hoped. Unforeseen obstacles lay in my path, and I found myself confronting my beliefs not only about my ability to teach but also about the very approach I was taking to help my students. Nothing could have prepared me for the miscommunication among guidance counselors, administrators, myself, and the students, or the struggles of teaching unsuccessful students to believe they have a chance. I had to define what success with big ideas meant to me and to my students despite the obstacles I faced and the conventional standards I struggled to meet.

BACKGROUND: MY SCHOOL SETTING AND PERSONAL AMBITIONS

I was apprehensive in starting my first official teaching job. I was fresh out of school, twenty-three years old, and entering a world of smug teenagers who couldn't care less about social studies. I did not want to portray my anxiety outwardly because I knew if I did, the students would eat me alive and my administrators would question my abilities. Being young, female, and petite, I have been constantly questioned about my ability to demonstrate authority with high school students. I knew I could do it, but I was anxious to prove it to everyone else. I was on a mission, a mission that only a young, idealistic teacher can have: I was going to motivate students to love social studies, teach them the skills to succeed in life, and prepare them to excel on the state social studies exam. I was armed with a bachelor's degree in history and a newly received teaching certificate from New York State. I believed that one of my biggest assets was my knowledge of the big idea concept. I was going to anchor every lesson and every unit with information that was relevant and interesting to my students. Feeling confident with my plan but trepidation about my limited experience, I walked into my classroom with mixed emotions.

I work in a charter school that draws students from both urban and suburban areas of western New York. The majority of my students come from middle- or low-income households. My classes are racially and ethnically diverse; I have almost an even distribution of African American and white students, with a few Latino students mixed in. I find this combination of students both exciting and challenging. Most of our families use our school as an alternative to urban public schools. We have a dress code, strict discipline policies, and a longer school day and year. The mission is to provide a private-like education for urban students and at no cost to the families. Since the beginning, I have been excited to teach my population of students; they are students that can benefit a great deal from me and from our school. The students have the option to succeed and excel, or to return to neighborhoods with little promise of upward social mobility. Most of them want to succeed, and I want to help them reach their goals.

My initial enthusiasm was tempered when I was given no curriculum other than the massive state global history and geography curriculum and no mentor. With the exception of the textbook, I was truly on my own. I liked some of the information in the textbook, but I did not like its organization, so I tried to use it as a tool rather than as a crutch. I wanted to incorporate big ideas, but I also wanted to survive from day to day, something that does not often result in innovative and ambitious teaching. So for the first semester, I put the big ideas on the back burner; I thought I would get around to them once I had more time and experience. Then, in my second semester of teaching, I was presented with a new option: another teacher and I would switch courses. He would teach my section of Global History II, and I would teach his Regents test preparation course to students who had previously failed the exam.

I was excited about the change because it seemed to me the perfect opportunity to start using big ideas. I was starting fresh with new students, students who needed a new way to learn global history. I saw this as my chance to try out big ideas in hopes that the students would find more success with the content if I could help them relate to it. I agreed to the change and started planning my strategies to help these three grade 11 students succeed on the New York State exam in June. I was jumping into a new experience with both excitement and anxiety. Would big ideas work? Could I really help these students pass the state exam? How would I deal with their Individual Educational Plans (IEPs) and special needs? I had many questions, though none seemed unanswerable.

A UNIQUE SET OF CHALLENGES: THE COURSE, THE TESTS, AND THE ADMINISTRATION

Big ideas were the first thing to come into my mind as I started planning for my new class. I knew I had three students, all had some sort of learning disability, and each had failed the global Regents exam twice. In New York State, the global exam is taken at the end of the students' sophomore year, after completing two year-long courses in world history. In grade 9, students cover prehistoric times through the late Middle Ages. Then in grade 10, students continue their chronological study, moving from the late Middle Ages through the present. The culmination of these courses is a three-hour state exam that tests them on material from both years of study. The test consists of fifty multiple-choice questions, five or six constructed-response questions, and two essays, one of which is a document-based question (DBQ). Needless to say, this is a great deal of information for students to remember. The global exam has the lowest pass rate of any Regents exam in our school. The previous year, only 55 percent of students passed the exam. Given this situation, the social studies faculty faced a great deal of pressure to improve scores. Our school's charter from New York State is renewed based on our test scores; therefore, our scores had to increase if we wanted to remain open. I felt the pressure, but I was convinced that this particular population of students would truly benefit from a course based in big ideas.

I met briefly with both the principal and the guidance counselor to discuss the students and the course. The guidance counselor made it clear to me that the main goal was to get these students to pass. She wanted them to graduate and to graduate on time. Her fear was that if they did not pass this exam in June, they would be doomed to be held back. June 2008 saw the graduation of our first senior class, and the administration wanted the highest graduation rate possible and for a high percentage of our students to be accepted into college.

At this time, I was told that the students would be taking the Regents Competency Test (RCT) in June, instead of the standard Regents exam, as a way to increase their likelihood of success and ultimately the likelihood of graduation. The RCT, which is being phased out, is set up much differently than the standard Regents exam. There is only one essay to write and the multiple-choice questions are relatively simple. I had no experience with the RCT exam; I had never even seen one. I expressed those concerns to the principal and both she and I agreed to search for old RCT exams in order to familiarize ourselves with the format. I searched online for copies of the test, and I relied on the principal to find hard copies. Despite this new and uncertain situation, I felt confident I could help these students to succeed on the test. I started my planning with big ideas on my mind.

For me, teaching with big ideas meant making history real for my students. Social studies teachers often hear about how the subject they teach is students' least favorite. Students report finding history boring and without relevance to their lives. I have always felt that if history could be presented in a way that related to students' lives and experiences, then social studies could be more than dates and dead political leaders; it could be human and interesting. I especially felt that this approach was what my struggling students needed. They needed to feel that history is tangible and approachable, and that they could be successful with the content. My goal was to show them that the events of the past and the events of the present are rooted in current ideas and emotions. If they could grasp the emotions and ideas behind history, then maybe they could make the connections the state exam expects of them. So I tried to think about how my students could relate their lives to the topics at hand. I intended to plan logically and personally so that I could cover as much content as possible while making that content personal to my students.

As I thought about the test preparation course, I realized that I did not have nearly enough time to cover the entire two years of curriculum in one semester. So my first order of business was to condense the material into essential units of study and then bring the units together through the use of big ideas. My plan was to have big ideas anchor each unit and lesson, and each big idea would be in the form of a question. I would have a main big idea for each unit, then use supplementary big idea questions for every class. I saw the students every other day for sixty-eight minutes per period. Because I wanted them to write, at least a little bit, every day, I decided that journaling was a good way to get them thinking, writing, and talking about ideas. I believed that structure and continuity were good ways to help the students feel more confident with the material, so I organized the classes as follows:

- Big idea question written on the board.
- Students enter class, read the big idea, then write a journal entry responding to the question.
- Class discussion of the question.
- Present the lesson—this is where I would present content to the students. Although it was material they were supposed to

have learned before, for the most part, it was new to them. My methods varied depending on the topic.

- Revisiting the big idea—here I led a class discussion of the big idea based on the material learned in the lesson.

After reviewing the material in the global history curriculum, I broke the semester down into nine units with about two weeks (about five classes) devoted to each topic. I broke my units down according to the material that seemed to appear most frequently on past exams (see table 3.1).

Since each unit consisted of only about five lessons, I believed the use of a big idea for each unit and lesson would allow both the students and me to approach a large amount of material in relevant and understandable ways. (See the example of Unit 1 in table 3.2.) I wanted them to take away the most essential ideas, but I also wanted them to relate those ideas and events to the present and to their own lives.

I knew the students coming into my class would struggle with basic reading and writing and that their confidence in their ability to succeed would be extremely low. These were students who constantly struggled in their other classes and on their exams. I anticipated their

Table 3.1.   Big Ideas for Regents Test Preparation

Unit	Big Idea
Unit 1: Geography and Culture	How does where you live affect how you live?
Unit 2: Greece and Rome	How have the thoughts of people of the past influenced the thoughts of people today?
Unit 3: World Religions	Why can religion lead to conflict and violence?
Unit 4: Africa	How does diversity affect the way people live?
Unit 5: Asia	What allows people to be successful and prosperous?
Unit 6: Europe and Latin America	How do people of different cultures influence one another?
Unit 7: Revolution and Industry	What is the difference between violent revolutions and nonviolent revolutions?
Unit 8: The World at War	How does war change people and societies?
Unit 9: Post-WWII	Why has the world become so interconnected?

Table 3.2. Unit 1: Geography and Culture

Topic	Big Idea
Day 1: World Geography and Features	How does where you live affect how you live?
Day 2: Defining Culture	How does culture make people who they are?
Day 3: Neolithic Revolution	What made the Neolithic Revolution revolutionary?
Day 4: River Valley Civilizations— Egypt and Mesopotamia	Why do people want to live near rivers?
Day 5: River Valley Civilizations— India and China	How does where you live affect how you live?

skepticism about my ability to help them succeed. So my goals for the course consisted not only of reviewing the material for the exam but also of strengthening their reading skills, writing skills, appreciation for social studies, and self-efficacy. I thought that if I could make world history relevant to them and show them that the struggles of the past are the same as the struggles today, they would find that information much easier to recall and use. Conventional methods had obviously not worked to help these students succeed, so I thought that big ideas could truly help them connect with history, and if they could connect with history, then their confidence in succeeding on the test would greatly increase.

SUCCESS AND STRUGGLES: WORKING WITH THE STUDENTS

The day finally came to start working with the students. I could not think about the class in the conventional way. It was not me teaching and them learning; it was all four of us working together to prepare for the exam. I only knew a small amount more about the RCT exam than they did. I had not been able to find any online copies of the RCT exam, and the principal had not yet delivered any news to me about her findings. All I was armed with were my big ideas and my plans. I approached the course like a workshop, all of us learning together.

As the students came in, the first thing I encountered was skepticism and uncertainty. They accepted my approach to the course and seemed responsive to working with me, but the big ideas took them off guard. I explained the purpose of big ideas to them and why I thought it was important for us to have these ideas to talk about in each class. I asked one of them to read aloud the question "Why do we need to study history?" I gave the class a few minutes to reflect, then I asked them what they thought. They did not seem to know how to respond, and for the first few weeks, this became the pattern: the students would come into class, read the big idea question, and stare off into space, waiting for me to tell them the answer. I tried prompting them, but I did not want them to think that I was going to give them the answers. They seemed not to want to think about the questions on their own. When I would encourage them to write something, they would often write "I don't know" or a brief sentence that merely restated the question. They seemed very reluctant to think for themselves.

And yet, although the students were slow to write responses, they seemed eager to talk about their ideas. I decided it was a good place to start. Beginning that first day, the discussions were productive and provided a good transition into the lessons. It took a good number of classes before the students felt comfortable with the big ideas, however. So I took notes about their responses and about the big idea questions; I reminded myself about what worked and what didn't, and what big ideas I wanted to repeat or try in a new way.

I discovered that the big ideas to which the students were most responsive were those that related to their lives. They struggled, however, to get past the idea that the content of social studies was not to be left in the social studies classroom. When we talked about the Scientific Revolution, they seemed surprised to hear names and ideas from science class; the scientific method, Copernicus, and Galileo did not seem like social studies content to them. These students were repeating many other subjects, so they often got much of their information confused. Consequently, it was not always easy to find effective big ideas. If they were too general or vague, the students were not always able to elaborate on their own ideas, or they provided vague responses. Sometimes I had to change the big idea question in the middle of class to make it more clear to the students or to give them more of a focus. For example, when I was discussing world religions, I presented the big idea "How does religion cause conflict?" The students seemed unsure what I meant by conflict. They wanted to discuss how parents want their children to go to church and remain celibate while the children do not want to comply with those religious norms. Although these points were on the right track, they were not exactly what I was looking for. I decided to ask "How can religion lead to conflict and violence?" The simple addition of the word "violence" led the students to talk about conflicts that exist between religions and cultures.

As a result, I found myself engaged in a process of creating a big idea, encouraging the students to discuss or write about their reactions to the idea, then helping them expand beyond their initial reactions. I would like to say that it was a science whose pattern I discovered, but in reality, it was trial and error every day. I was constantly modifying my approach.

It wasn't until the beginning of March that the students really started to engage with the big ideas. One of the first questions that really got the students motivated was "Why do people believe in and participate in religion?" By this point, they felt comfortable writing every class and putting their ideas into the journal entries, but this was the first time I really saw the spark of interest. They came into class, got settled, and immediately started to write. It appeared to be a topic they could understand. Their written entries were tentative and simple, but I felt encouraged that they were grasping and participating with the ideas. For example, one of the students wrote about how "people take religion real personal" and continued on to say that people need religion to give them hope and guidance. This entry prompted a discussion about how there are many different religions, especially in the United States, and that the desire to practice religion transcends cultures and societies. Their journal entries had transitioned from consisting of a single sentence or "I don't know" to paragraphs of four or five sentences. Our conversations had also transitioned: They had started as short answers to my prompting questions; now I acted as a participant in the conversations with the students taking more of the lead.

I felt inspired; the big ideas were starting to have the effect I hoped they would. The students engaged with the material and began relating to it by inserting anecdotes from their lives. For example, during a discussion about governments and their effects on society, one of the students said her father was complaining about jobs going to China and how our government needs to do more to get jobs for Americans.

The students' participation increased as the month continued. In my journal entry on March 19, I noted that "the kids are getting much more into big ideas. Instead of trying to get me to do all the talking, they have responses right away. They are drawing on their studies in other courses (U.S. history) and relating those ideas to global history." I noticed that they started to express pride in their answers and seemed less apprehensive about participating. Their body language changed and their comments became much more positive. They came into class and instead of talking about the latest gossip around school, they talked about the big idea or started writing in their journals. They kept their heads up instead of down on their desks. They sought out information from textbooks, the Internet, or other sources I had available. Overall, their confidence with the subject seemed to grow.

The big ideas also prompted discussions about topics beyond our scope of study. At first, I was reluctant to get too far off task, but as their questions became in-depth and thoughtful, I remembered my goals of helping them improve their life skills and appreciation of social studies. In April, one of our big idea questions was "What makes a society stable and successful?" One of my students came in and, even before she took her seat, said, "I have an answer to that question!" She sat down right away and began writing her journal entry. This question prompted a student-initiated discussion on world population and how a large population can be a detriment to society. One of the students even went over to a computer to look up population sizes of countries around the world. They were interested and motivated to find out more. Although our lesson did not center on world population sizes, I could not hold them back from learning more about the topic.

As the semester started to wind down, I was feeling very encouraged about the progress we had made. I had still not found any tangible resources on the RCT exam, nor had the principal, but I was optimistic nonetheless. I was using old Regents exam questions to help prepare them and working with them on their essay-writing skills. I felt sure that their confidence had grown, their writing skills had improved, and their familiarity with exam-type questions had increased. Our class was not without struggles. Attendance issues, meeting the students' IEP needs, and reading comprehension all continued to challenge us. Yet none of these problems seemed insurmountable until the end of the semester, when an abrupt change took the wind out of our sails.

OUR SUCCESS DERAILED

With a week to go before the June exams, the students and I were feeling confident. We were working on test preparation and coming up with strategies to help them succeed. I had told the students everything I knew about the RCT. I told them that they only had to write one essay. They were confident in their abilities to pass the test, partly because they knew it was a modified version of the Regents exam. When I told the students that they would not have a document-based question and that they would have their choice of essays on the RCT, they seemed relieved. All three students said that writing essays was what they were most apprehensive about. They expressed how much better they felt in being able to choose which topic they wrote about. I gave them as many test-taking tools as possible; we even made an exam schedule together where they charted which exams they had to take on which days and when the review sessions were held.

At the beginning of class a week before the exam, one of my students came in very upset. She said that the guidance counselor had told her that she was going to be taking the regular Regents exam in global history next week, and if she failed that, then she would be taking the RCT exam. My student was upset because she was afraid to fail the Regents exam. She said that she didn't feel prepared for the Regents exam and that she would feel horrible if she failed again. All she wanted to do was take the RCT. I told her that I had not heard that she had to take the Regents exam but that I would find out. I called the guidance counselor to come and speak to all of us. The counselor came into class and relayed the news that she wanted the students to try to pass the Regents exam, and if they failed, then they could take the RCT. She said that they should push themselves to pass the Regents, since that was the "better" exam to pass.

I was upset and my students could see it. They were upset and feeling defeated. They expressed anger that they were just being informed about taking the Regents exam. They said that they did not think it was fair because they were not ready. I agreed with them but knew it would not be wise to imply that I didn't think they could pass the Regents exam. I remember one student asking me, "Why do they make us keep taking this test? It's like they want to make us feel stupid." Given this new circumstance, I wanted to have some words of encouragement, but I could only empathize with my students and tell them I would help as much as I could. But they were lost to me after this news. All the fear and doubt I had worked so hard to rid them of was back.

That five-minute conversation trumped five months of work. I wanted to yell and scream that it wasn't fair, but I was in an odd situation: I did not want my students to think that I believed they couldn't pass the Regents exam. After all, most of the review material we had been using was geared toward the Regents exam. I asked the guidance counselor to stay with the class and I went to talk to the principal. I told her of my frustration and anger that I had not been made aware of this situation before the students. She said that it was the plan all along and that I must have misinterpreted the purpose of the course. I felt confused about why she and I had worked so hard to find information on the RCT exam when she really wanted them to be preparing for the Regents exam. I doubted myself and what we had discussed. I told her that I felt the students would be more successful if we just had them take the RCT, but she would not have that. She wanted the students to take the exam in hopes that they would pass. She said she felt that my preparing them this past semester was enough and that we might as well see how they would do. She added, "We need to give them another chance to take the real exam. You never know; they may just pass."

I could not make her see that by doing that, she was setting them up to fail. I also did not want to say I felt sure they would fail, because that would not have reflected well on my confidence in the students. I felt ashamed that I had not prepared them well enough for the assessments they needed to take. I had had the mindset for the entire semester that they would be taking the RCT, so I thought they would be adequately prepared to pass. Once I learned that they were taking the more challenging Regents exam, I felt unsure that I had done enough. I was apprehensive about them having to deal with a document-based question when we had not spent any time reviewing the format. I felt like giving up.

I went back to class and tried to reassure the students that it was going to be fine, and that they were prepared for both exams. The students reacted with frustration and defeat. They seemed almost as if they were resigned to fail. They did not yell or get outwardly upset, but I could tell by their expressions and body language that their confidence was shattered. I reassured them as best I could, we rewrote our exam calendars, and they went on their way.

A week later, all three students failed the Regents exam and then the RCT. I was crushed. I felt that we had worked so hard and made so much progress. The students did not seem surprised. When I spoke with one after the exam, she said she felt she could never pass the global history exam no matter what she did. She added, "I never really thought I was going to pass. I always fail exams. I'm not taking it again." It was disappointing because not long ago she had been enthusiastic and interested. Now she seemed even more defeated than when the class started.

No other teachers or administrators blamed me for the students' exam results; I think they expected them to fail anyway. But I blamed myself. I questioned my methods and my approach to the course. I spent a good amount of time going over my notes and plans, contemplating what I could have done differently. In the end, I decided that where I felt the most successful was when we were discussing big ideas, and I started to believe that those conversations generated much more confidence in my students than any graphic organizers, notes, or test reviews we attempted. I decided not to judge my success on the state exams but on the changes I saw from January to June. Doing so may help me get through the day, but I wondered if it would be enough to help me keep my job. With so much riding on test scores and graduation rates, could I really judge success in any other way? I may not know the answers to these questions right away, but hopefully with experience will come enlightenment.

WHAT I LEARNED AND MY HOPE FOR BIG IDEAS

My initial hopes were that the students would be able to use big ideas as a way to bring history alive. Was my goal achieved? That depends on what ends I assess. If I look at their exam scores, no, my goals with big ideas were not achieved. The students did not do better on the exam because I focused my lessons on big ideas. But if I focus on another end, their responses and participation in class by the end of the semester, then yes, using big ideas was very successful. The students started to think for themselves; they did not wait for me to tell them what to think. They told me stories from their own lives that related to topics of government, society, or economics; they talked about how topics of religion or politics related to their beliefs and experiences. I could see that they were invested and interested in the material because they spoke about history being evident in their lives. They did not rely on guided worksheets on which all their answers were merely copied from a book. Their journal entries expressed their thoughts, prompted only by a question unlikely to be found in a textbook. Instead of sitting mindlessly and copying down notes from an overhead, my students researched information on their own, asked questions, and found their own answers. They were active learners engaged in the material.

I found that I was excited to try out my big ideas in each class. I was anxious to hear what they would say and how they could relate to the material. I then found it much easier to incorporate big ideas into my grade 9 global history classes. I was able to take units on the Middle Ages in Europe or the religion of Islam and formulate big ideas that I would not have considered in the past. I began planning my units around big ideas like "What made the Dark Ages dark?" My self-efficacy had improved along with that of my students. I felt encouraged that I could make history meaningful for my students, and that ancient history did not have to be dull and lifeless. I was able to see themes and trends in history much more easily once I had opened my mind to big ideas. I was no longer confined to the textbook or the state curriculum, and it was liberating. In the beginning of the year, I felt as if I were drowning and the textbook was my life preserver; by the end, I was confident enough to form a curriculum on my own, taking pieces from many different sources and weaving them together with big ideas.

I try not to think of my three students in the RCT prep course as my guinea pigs, but they did help me learn how to find my own style of teaching. They gave me hope for teaching with big ideas and gave me the confidence to move out of my comfort zone. Although they, and I, were not conventionally successful, I know that my teaching is better because of my experience with them. I can only hope that their minds have been opened and their skills have improved because of working with me.

4

FROM THE HOLOCAUST TO DARFUR: TEACHING ABOUT GENOCIDE

Joseph Karb and Andrew Beiter

My responsibility as a teacher is to try to help my students to be good people. And good people work to make the right choices and work against evil.

—Paul Tobias

Of all the big ideas that can be taught in social studies, one could argue that teaching students to value each other as human beings is perhaps the most important. Whether it is in appreciating diversity, understanding our shared humanity, or seeing that civilization is fragile, this concept is at the heart of who we are as a society and as educators.

Although man's inhumanity to man is as old as Cain and Abel, advances in technology have made it more widespread and potent, allowing our time to be labeled an age of genocide. From Armenia to Darfur, the track record of humanity's darker impulses is painfully evident. The task for us as educators is how to teach it, and to use its lessons for the betterment of all.

It is with this background in mind that we wrote this chapter. In order to teach our students to be good, we have the obligation to help them develop their own understandings of where and why society has fallen off the tracks. As noble as these goals are, however, they are difficult to put into practice. We teach, after all, in an imperfect world that is rife with obstacles, roadblocks, and constraints. Standardized assessments, teacher in-service days, and snow days all chip away at the time we have with our students.

Given that our readers likely face similar circumstances, our intent is not to pretend that these obstacles don't exist, but instead to acknowledge, understand, and even embrace them as a way of advancing our profession. No worthy goal is ever reached without working around challenges that emerge; teaching is no different. In fact, knowing that these impediments exist is important, for that knowledge allows us to prepare and react accordingly.

With these several points in mind, we share our story of teaching about the Holocaust to grade 8 students in New York State. While on one level we will offer lesson ideas and our experiences, on another we will describe the challenges and setbacks that surfaced as we worked toward our big idea goal of teaching students how to recognize the causes of genocide.

THE ELEPHANT IN THE ROOM: THE STATE ASSESSMENT

Although our motivation for genocide education is clear, the constraints created by the New York State curriculum cannot be ignored. In teaching any unit, one must consider the guidelines created through the state standards and curriculum. These standards include five core social studies areas:

- History of the United States and New York
- World history
- Geography
- Economics
- Civics, citizenship, and government

For each of these standards, the state curriculum developers created learning outcomes that students should master throughout their social studies career, along with a core curriculum guide which details the major people, places, and events on which students can be tested. This core curriculum for grades 7 and 8 is ultimately assessed with a statewide test that measures how well our students have learned U.S. history and geography at the end of grade 8.

The state assessment comprises multiple-choice questions and a document-based question (DBQ) essay as well as a number of constructed-response questions. The essay and multiple-choice items can be on anything from the grades 7–8 curriculum—a challenge in itself, considering the amount of possible content, which totals fifty-one single-spaced pages.

Although the scores from this assessment do not determine if students pass the course, they are used to evaluate the effectiveness of the social studies program at a school. Consequently, administrators and many teachers create significant pressure on themselves and on students to produce high test scores. Additionally, instructional time becomes an issue because many teachers spend anywhere from two to eight weeks at the end of the grade 8 year in test preparation.

Because anything from the state curriculum can be on the exam, many teachers believe they need to cover everything, so they feel limited in examining topics in greater detail. One such topic is the Holocaust. The New York State curriculum for grade 8 social studies includes only a twenty-five-word list of topics related to the Holocaust and the study of genocide:

> The Nazi Holocaust—Hitler's "Final Solution"; worldwide horror; human rights violations; United States response to the Holocaust: the displaced persons camp at Fort Ontario, Oswego, New York; the Nuremberg Trials.

This document is not designed to be all inclusive, but it seems strange to us that an event which can teach students so much about life is given only cursory attention. This brief mention—coupled with the pressure of the state assessment—results in many teachers spending less than one day on the Holocaust in their race to cover everything else.

Of course, teachers can adjust their schedules and customize their curriculum based on their areas of strength. But with the increased emphasis on state assessments, the flexibility once enjoyed by teachers seems to be diminishing. It can become difficult justifying spending two weeks on a topic that might yield one multiple-choice question on the assessment. However, teachers do have a responsibility to be more than assessment robots and to teach lessons that will impact students' views of the world.

During our first years of teaching, we were fortunate to have a curriculum director who encouraged the practice of "courageous deletion." She always said that we should cover a little less content in more detail rather than try to skim everything. Her point was that teaching students to have a deeper understanding of the essential topics would more than compensate for them missing an occasional question on a minute detail.

Still concerned that our test scores might be impacted, our faculty went on to analyze the patterns of the multiple-choice questions on the previous years' exams. We found that the pattern reinforced her thesis: specifically, that we could feel comfortable not covering parts of our curriculum because the state test developers consistently ignored certain sections of the course curriculum. We concluded that, if the test questions emphasized certain items over others, we had the liberty to focus on big ideas that would impact students in a significant way. One such case is our study of the Holocaust and genocide.

A RECIPE FOR GENOCIDE: WHY DOES MASS MURDER OCCUR AND HOW CAN IT BE STOPPED?

All too often, social studies teachers present the cruelty of the Holocaust as an isolated event. These units focus on Hitler, gas chambers, and war crimes, and they end with a defiant "Never again!" Covering mass murder in this way is laudable but, ultimately, might not go as far as it could. For if we really want to empower our students to prevent future genocides, we must look beyond the facts alone to the larger lessons these horrific events can teach us.

As an initial caution, it goes without saying that the Holocaust is an event like few others in human history, one that educators and the general public should understand and draw lessons from. Most cursory analogies to the Holocaust—or Hitler—are inaccurate and should be attempted with a great deal of care. The Holocaust and other genocides are uniquely specific historical events, yet when they are looked at as a whole, similarities can surface. More importantly, when these shared characteristics are understood, they can make significant and lasting differences in how students approach the world.

So with this unit, we wanted to expand the topic of the Holocaust to include a comparative study of other genocides, and thus examine their similarities and differences. The Holocaust, after all, is unfortunately not a singular event. In nearly every decade of the twentieth century and now the twenty-first, mass killings around the world have claimed millions of lives. Ignoring these other genocides borders on educational malpractice, for there is much to be learned from studying them. The situations in Armenia, Rwanda, Cambodia, and Darfur have similarities that should not be ignored.

This approach, of course, opens up a massive area of analysis, one that is not necessarily student friendly. We therefore wanted to create a means for our students to comprehend these shared characteristics in a way that was age appropriate. The result: our big idea of constructing a "recipe" for genocide. The idea of a *recipe* provided us with a way to help students understand the early warning signs of mass murder so that they would be better equipped to prevent such occurrences in the future. Doing so would hopefully inspire them not to be bystanders to any similar cruelty, both in the world and in their daily lives. After all, Rwandan President Paul Kagame notes, "people can be made to be bad, and they can also be taught to be good."

OUR STUDENTS AND OURSELVES

The Holocaust has always been an area of interest and focus during our collective twenty years of teaching grade 8 social studies. During this time, we have experimented with various approaches, leading to the evolution of the recipe concept. Over a two-week period in the spring of 2007, we taught the unit to 160 grade 8 students in a rural school district located in western New York. The student population is 99 percent European American, with a majority of students falling into a middle or lower socioeconomic category; roughly 15 percent of our students are classified as needing special education services.

We both teach five grade 8 classes, with an average of nineteen students in each. Each class went through the same sequence of activities. We created this unit together and implemented it on a similar schedule so we could better understand what was happening in our classrooms. Of course, since every teacher and class is unique, there were minor differences in the lessons when they were implemented. As we both have integrated schedules, our special education colleague assisted by helping our students focus and understand important concepts.

OUR CHALLENGES

Outside the constraints of the state assessment, teaching about genocide had a whole different set of challenges that most regular units do not, namely, a very sensitive subject matter coupled with imagery and symbolism that could disturb some students or, worse, could be darkly appealing to a few. Specifically, we dealt with challenges involving the need to account for the emotional shock value of genocide, the need to physically involve students with the lessons, and the need to help our students make sense of the sheer numbers involved.

We never try to hook our students with a horrific image from a Nazi death camp or spend too much time sharing images of Hitler or swastikas. Obviously, teaching *any* portion of the Holocaust involves introducing our students to these things, but to dwell on them prevents learners from going beyond being horrified to understanding why the event happened.

Another initial problem is the difficulty of getting students physically involved with this topic. The dominant thrust of our teaching has always been to dramatically engage students in what they are studying. For example, when we study immigration, our students spend a day at a fictitious Ellis Island. When we teach the Great Depression, students dress up as hobos at an outdoor soup kitchen. Based on Howard Gardner's theory of multiple intelligences, this student-centered, active approach capitalizes on the many different strengths our students bring to the classroom.

But to teach the Holocaust in such an active way poses some immediate and possibly repugnant concerns. To dress up some of our students as Jews and others as Nazis not only violates the dignity of the victims but puts our students in a difficult situation. Moreover, the teacher may be liable for disciplinary action or dismissal—as has happened in several districts around North America.

Likewise, to assemble a group of students in an imaginary railcar is too sensitive a scenario to replicate. So how, then, can one teach the Holocaust in ways that involve students in what they are learning? The answer is that, like anything else, one must be careful. *Not* teaching about this event is unthinkable, so we have found that, with a little planning and creativity, we can advance our big idea without putting ourselves or our students at risk.

To deal with these challenges, we began our unit with an event that set the stage for the Holocaust but is without any of the concerns described above: the Treaty of Versailles.

OUR UNIT

We started our unit with an active hook centering on our Treaty of Versailles simulation. On days 1–6, we attempted to create a sense of empathy in our students as well as give them a basic understanding of the causes of the Holocaust. In the remaining lessons, we concentrated on the questions "Why did this happen?" and "What can we learn from the Holocaust?" The unit culminated in the "Recipe for Genocide" and a genocide project.

Days 1–2: The Treaty of Versailles

One of the most significant ingredients in a recipe for creating genocide is a society in turmoil. It is difficult to understand the Holocaust without going back to the 1919 Treaty of Versailles. Following World War I, the victorious Allied Powers promised Germany a fair treatment. At Versailles, however, the Allies set a fine of $33 billion and took all of Germany's colonies, valuable lands, and armaments. These actions triggered the vengeful rise of Hitler and the Nazi party, who blamed Germany's economic depression on the "Jews and international back-stabbers" at Versailles. Given that the Holocaust is hard to imagine without this backdrop, it is important to assist our students in understanding the treaty and its ramifications.

Because a peace conference is an event that lends itself nicely to an active learning situation, we divided our students into groups representing the "big four" countries at Versailles: France, Great Britain, Italy, and the United States. In order to involve all our students, we then set up several tables in which the treaty negotiations would take place. (We actually do three separate treaty negotiations at the same time, depending on class size.) After studying on Day 1 what their respective countries wanted from Germany, each bargaining team divided Germany's possessions up in Day 2. One student in each class role-played an angry Kaiser Wilhelm. Asked how he felt about the ensuing peace treaty, the student-Kaiser invariably said, "I am outraged, and this will set the stage for another war!"

In setting the stage for the rise of World War II, we like this simulation because it introduces the students to the prevailing German perspective on Versailles—without putting them in the situation of impersonating a Nazi. Likewise, this lesson also provides a much needed hook into the unit. More importantly, if the students can understand why the Germans were angry at Versailles, they can better understand their need for a scapegoat in the Jewish people and others twenty years later. In doing so, students identify a key psychological part of the recipe for genocide.

At the end of the period, the students responded to the question of how Versailles might be connected to World War II. Although the majority of their responses indicated a deeper understanding of the role that revenge and national humiliation played in the rise of Hitler, like any class with any subject, a few students seemed unable to understand that connection. However, the majority of the class offered thoughtful answers such as "The Germans were mad at the Allies and wanted to get even" and "They [the Germans] were looking for someone to blame for their problems." To further assess these comments, we asked students to complete a homework worksheet on Versailles that analyzed the impact of the treaty on the German society and economy.

Day 3: Introduction to the Holocaust

Now that students were beginning to understand the psyche of the German people, we thought about how to get them to understand how the victims felt, without having to persecute them in class. To do so requires some obvious sensitivity, especially if there are students of Jewish ancestry present.

So to start Day 3—the actual introduction to the Holocaust—we began our class by handing out three-by-five cards to students as they walked in. Before discussing any Holocaust-related details, we asked them to imagine that they had to leave their house on a day's notice, taking with them only a single suitcase full of items and clothing. What sentimental item of theirs (not iPods, cell phones, etc.), we asked, would they bring? They wrote these items down on the cards and placed them in a 10 by 5 foot taped-off rectangle that we had marked on the floor. What they did not know was that the shape replicated the outline of a cattle car, the typical transport used by the Nazis for their victims.

Once they completed this task, we introduced the situation in Germany in 1939: twenty years after the Treaty of Versailles, Adolph Hitler and the Nazi party have mobilized the anger of the German people and have begun deporting their enemies to concentration camps in cattle cars. Although 6 million of the ultimate victims were Jews, roughly 5 million more were other enemies of the Nazi state—Poles, trade unionists, Gypsies, homosexuals, religious leaders, and prisoners of war.

After explaining this scenario, we played the brief railcar scene from the movie *Escape from Sobibor*. By putting the students' three-by-five cards in the rectangle—rather than on their persons—we mitigated some of our concern about active learning and the Holocaust. For after the movie clip ended, the students realized that something important of theirs was in the cattle car en route to a concentration camp, without them actually *being* in the rectangle. And while one or two cards per class were off topic or sarcastic (and were quietly ignored), the majority of the students made some thoughtful connections. One commented, "The cards made me see that they [the deported victims] were real people just like me." With this realization, we finished the lesson with some notes and readings on the basic facts and geography of the Holocaust.

Combined with the lesson on the Treaty of Versailles, the experience of the deportations introduced our students to another key component of the recipe for genocide, namely, that the technology of the twentieth century—such as railroads—enhanced the ability of the perpetrators to inflict harm. The students were also physically and psychologically hooked on what they were studying, though in a manner that was neither insensitive nor inflammatory. We make these claims based on our observations of how focused our students were and on the number of questions each class asked. To further assess these reactions, we asked our students to write a one-page essay reflecting on what the activity meant to them.

From this point on, we found it important to connect our daily lessons with the big idea. Now that our students were hooked both emotionally and physically, we felt it was time to encourage them to think about what they were learning and how it was linked to the recipe for genocide. To do this, we utilized a list that we put on the front board in order to begin compiling the causes of the Holocaust. Some of the students' responses included recipe items of "a weak government," "people looking for a scapegoat," and "railroads and poison gas made it easier to kill more people." Throughout the unit, we added to this list after each lesson. Eventually, we used this list as the basis for our comparative study of other genocides.

Day 4: The Causes of the Holocaust

Given the student interest created in the first three days, we were able to spend Day 4 focusing on notes, video, and readings on the causes of the Holocaust. To engage the students in this lesson, we started with an account of a survivor's testimony that included many of the key terms we wanted to emphasize—crematorium, gas chamber, Final Solution, deportation. After a discussion of these ideas, we transitioned them into some notes, which were presented in an outlined, closed format, concentrating on basic terminology, vocabulary, and geography. We ended this lesson with a visual reinforcement from the ABC News video series *The Century*, which reiterated some of these basic facts. While very factual in nature, such media allowed the material to be retaught in a manner more appealing for visual learners.

Day 5: The Numbers of the Holocaust

We also found that teaching about genocide involves another major concern: the numbers of the event—that is, how to introduce 11 million victims such that a thirteen-year-old might take their deaths to heart. For in order to care about the causes of genocide and our big idea, students need to have a personal understanding of its scope.

To teach the numbers of the Holocaust, we had to scale that big number down to one—in other words, *one* student relating to *one* victim, thus making the incomprehensible tangible. It was Joseph Stalin, after all, who approached this problem with the cynical observation that "a million deaths is a statistic—but a single death is a tragedy." We have to admit that, from a teaching perspective, he was right: it is impossible to learn about the Holocaust or any genocide without making it personal.

It was at this point that our big idea of teaching the recipe for genocide collided head-on with the event itself. How could we get an adolescent to care about an event that happened sixty years ago, in black and white, to victims he or she will never meet? The answer was to introduce each of our students to a victim.

We found a lesson through the United States Holocaust Memorial Museum that focused on the same theme. Printing twenty-five victim profiles from their Web site, we asked each of our students to retrieve one of these sheets from a container, symbolizing the inhumanity of the Nazi death machine.

With poignant music playing in the background and eleven candles lit, each student silently read the brief biography of one of the Holocaust's victims, then completed a short worksheet focusing on the victim's life. The stories contained brief life histories of the Holocaust victims, including family information, personal stories, and how they were eventually killed. (These victim profiles can be found at the Holocaust Museum's Web site, www.ushmm.org/education/foreducators/resource/pdf/idcards.pdf). Afterward, we asked the students to "introduce" their victims to a person sitting next to them.

The students reacted in serious and somber ways, seeming to internalize the power of the activity. "What we did today made me see that they were people too," said a student. Later, another student noted, "Class was very sad today—how could this have happened?"

We continued the activity by asking students to compute how many of their middle school peers would have to be involved in such a death count by having them divide the figure of 11 million by the 600 students at our school. In doing so, we laid the psychological framework for caring about genocide, which we found paid educational dividends when we introduced more of the recipe.

We ended the numbers lesson with some images of Auschwitz and then helped our students prepare questions for an Auschwitz survivor, Joseph Diamond, scheduled to visit the next day. Our purpose for combining the numbers with a survivor was to help students understand and care about the causes of genocide and, by extension, our instructional activity around the recipe for genocide.

Day 6: Holocaust Survivor—Joseph Diamond
Due to Mr. Diamond's age, it was imperative that he make only one presentation to our grade 8 students. Doing so, however, presented

some scheduling problems. Although almost no one would argue against the educational value of hearing a Holocaust survivor, fitting our speaker into the schedule of our middle school was an obstacle we did not anticipate. After all, squeezing any speaker or assembly into a busy school is like introducing a bill in Congress! Our colleagues were for it as long as it did not take *their* class time. After some creative scheduling, cajoling, and deal making, we finally found a way to fit Mr. Diamond's one-hour speech into the grade 8 schedule.

Our efforts were rewarded by seeing the wonderful effect that his speech had on our students. "Mr. Diamond made the Holocaust real to me. It's one thing to read about it in a book—another to hear about it firsthand," said one. Another remarked, "He made me realize that I shouldn't be a bystander here at school." Mr. Diamond's testimony also reinforced several key ingredients of the recipe, such as ethnic hatred and economic instability. Just as importantly, he raised the interest level of our students so that we could more easily teach the topic in greater detail. There were times at the beginning of this unit when students displayed some nervous and childish laughter. The power of Mr. Diamond's testimony, however, made for a very emotional and engaging experience, one that seemed to embrace all of our students.

Day 7: Bystanders and Resisters, the Holocaust and Bullying

Equally important elements of the recipe for genocide are the actions of bystanders, who know that what is happening is wrong and do nothing, and resisters, who attempt to help those being victimized. Mr. Diamond's presentation set the stage for a discussion of bystanders, resisters, and how the Holocaust relates to our students' own lives. For this lesson, we asked the school counselors to join us for the day to help us connect the idea of Holocaust bystanders and resisters to the issue of bullying in school. We thought it important to make immediate and real-world connections to the students' lives.

This lesson began with a debriefing of the survivor presentation and the question of what we could add to our recipe for genocide. Typically students focused on the role of bystanders, adding insights such as, "Genocides can happen when good people do nothing," and "There are always people who ignore what is happening."

After the idea of "Don't be a bystander" was identified by the students, we transitioned to the role of bystanders and resisters during the Holocaust. We briefly introduced resisters like Irena Sendler and Oskar Schindler and we asked the students to analyze the famous poem by the German priest Martin Niemoller:

> They came for the Communists, and I didn't object—For I wasn't a Communist;
> They came for the Socialists, and I didn't object—For I wasn't a Socialist;
> They came for the labor leaders, and I didn't object—For I wasn't a labor leader;
> They came for the Jews, and I didn't object—For I wasn't a Jew;
> Then they came for me—And there was no one left to object.

Reflecting on the poem, we asked students how the idea of bystander and resister is related to their own lives in school. In other words, we inquired, were there situations where they found themselves remaining silent while something bad was happening to someone else, and were there times when they actively helped a fellow student in need? The students very quickly gave the example of bullying, which we anticipated, given that Mr. Diamond mentioned this in his speech. We then turned the class over to the counselor, who discussed bullying with students, linking it to the Holocaust through the following questions:

- What were the characteristics of bullies, bystanders, and resisters during the Holocaust?
- What are the characteristics of bullies, bystanders, and resisters at school?
- What are some strategies to prevent and stop bullying when it occurs?

We then discussed the question "Will we ever really know the impact a resister can have?"

The idea of preventing suicide, changing a life, and preventing future violence was discussed. Students developed a number of hypothetical "what if" questions that highlighted the importance of bystanders and resisters.

At the end of class, we watched the last few minutes of *Schindler's List*, in which Schindler Jews and their descendents placed a memory stone on Oskar Schindler's grave. The reaction of the students was moving; one could hear a pin drop in the room, and a number of students had tears in their eyes. Before the students left class, we asked them to write on a three-by-five card one thing we can learn from the Holocaust. All relevant, they included:

- "Don't always follow the crowd."
- "Stand up for people."
- "No matter how you were treated, have compassion."
- "Only we can prevent another holocaust."
- "Don't be a bystander. If someone is fighting or doing drugs, you should stop them before they get hurt."

This lesson created a connection between the Holocaust and what goes on in the hallways of a typical school. With this lesson, we encouraged students to resist cruelty in any form. By making the terms *bystander* and *resister* a part of their vocabulary, our lesson was able to extend the lessons of the Holocaust into their day-to-day lives.

Days 8–9: Genocide Learning Stations
Thus far, each class of students had created a list of what they believed should be included in the Recipe for Genocide based on their study of the Holocaust. The lists included ten to twelve items, such as hatred of a group, discrimination, scapegoating, economic depression, perpetrators, propaganda, transportation, and communication network. Although each item was discussed when it was placed on the list, we had not discussed the lists as a whole. Therefore, on Day 8, we asked the students to discuss and compare the differences between class lists. Some recipes tended to focus on items we

expected—such as the perpetrator's use of technology—while others concentrated on the role of bystanders.

Over Days 8–9, students worked in small groups, visiting genocide learning stations on Armenia, Cambodia, Rwanda, and Darfur. Each learning station featured a poster with basic information and photographs and a short video or radio story. Students visited each station for 10–15 minutes, during which they used the Recipe for Genocide list to look for similarities and differences between genocides. The end product for each group was a revised Recipe for Genocide that included at least five conditions that seemed to be present during most genocides. Students had to support their choices based on information gleaned from the learning stations and were assigned a short presentation which asked them to describe the major causes—or ingredients—of the genocides they studied.

Day 10: Genocide Project

Given the classroom activities over the preceding two weeks, we believed it was important to allow the students to dig deeper into an area of this unit in which they had a special interest. In doing so, we offered them an opportunity to reflect upon what they learned and to take advantage of a creative outlet to express their new understandings. Given the theory of multiple intelligences, we thought it was important to provide the students with options that utilized their inherent strengths. Some of these options are listed in the appendix to this chapter.

Day 11: Unit Test Review

To prepare for the final assessment, students used this class to review the material on the Holocaust and the key components of the recipe. They completed review sheets, saw a summary video, and wrote down their reactions to the following questions on a three-by-five card: "Why is studying the Holocaust important?" and "What are the warning signs that genocide might happen?"

As teachers, we found that the responses from this brief activity were especially gratifying. One student wrote, "Studying the Holocaust and other genocides made me realize that it can happen again and that it's important for all of us to know what to look for." This response captured the essence of our instructional plan, one that indicates that the student understood the material but, more importantly, is on the path to understanding the warning signs of mass murder.

Day 12: Unit Test on the Holocaust and Genocide Studies
Students took a traditional multiple-choice, fill-in-the-blanks unit test that also asked them to write a short essay discussing the following question: "What are the warning signs of genocide that you learned from the Holocaust—in other words, what are the *ingredients* to genocide—and why is it important that they are understood?"

CONCLUSION

The students' answers to the essay question were very satisfying, with many of them eagerly describing several of the ingredients of genocide. Their responses also indicated a broad understanding of why studying the Holocaust is important, one that reflects the social awareness and moral leadership so important to our pluralistic society. And while our teaching of this big idea unit was not easy, perfect, or complete, we hope that it offered an opportunity for our students to see their world differently, appreciate that it is fragile, and most importantly, to speak up when it is at risk.

APPENDIX: HOLOCAUST PROJECT OPTIONS

For Students Who Like to Write

Option A: Essay
Write an essay that discusses the following:

- What was the Holocaust?
- When, why, and where did it happen?
- What were its causes?
- Whom did it involve?

- What can it teach us about how to live today?
- Why is it important that the world remember?

Length: at least 7 paragraphs, preferably typed.

Option B: Short Story

Create a fictional story that depicts one or more aspects of the Holocaust. This story should:

- Be *original*—not a retelling of another story or testimony that you have heard.
- Have interesting and realistic characters and plot.
- Prove a point or teach a lesson about what the Holocaust was about.

Length: at least 3 pages typed, and with a title, cover page, and maybe even some pictures.

Option C: Poetry

Write a poem that:

- Discusses the basics of the Holocaust and its lessons for the world today, or focuses on a certain aspect that learners are interested in.
- Proves a point—relate it to the Holocaust and express emotions.

Length: at least 40 lines. (A line should include at least four words.) The poem does not have to rhyme. It should be typed and maybe even decorated with some pictures.

Option D: Research Paper

Write a short research paper (2–3 pages typed) on the genocide happening recently in Darfur, a part of the African country called Sudan. The paper should discuss what has happened, why it should be considered a genocide, and what potentially can be done to stop it. Go to www.ushmm.org/conscience/alert/darfur/ for more details and links. This report should also include some pictures of Darfur.

For Students Who Like to Use Their Artistic Talents

Option E: Drawing

Draw or create a serious work of art that describes the Holocaust. This picture should:

- Be at least 10 by 20 inches in size.
- Use watercolor, charcoal, or pastels—but no markers or colored pencils.
- Have a brief, one-paragraph description of the point you are trying to make about the Holocaust.
- Be moving and artistically done.

Please note: drawings of Hitler or swastikas are not recommended.

Option F: Poster or Collage Memorial Dedicated to Life

After studying the Holocaust, most people are moved to better appreciate the things they have, such as their life, family, friends, or even a warm meal or bed. This poster/collage should:

- Be completed on a large piece of poster board.
- Use your own drawings and/or pictures from magazines or the Internet, some of which could deal with the Holocaust, but not necessarily.
- Have a title.
- Make its viewer appreciate life more.
- Be dedicated to the victims of the Holocaust.
- Be neatly done and loaded with pictures and words such as "Life," "Love," "Appreciation," and the like.

Option G: Poster or Collage Memorial Dedicated to Tolerance

Because a major cause of the Holocaust was stereotyping, create a poster that encourages your viewers to be more tolerant of those who are different. It should follow all the guidelines outlined in Option F above.

For Students Who Like to Express Their Creativity in Different Ways

Option H: Memorial Book to Kristallnacht

Kristallnacht was the destruction of hundreds of Jewish businesses and over 1,500 synagogues in 1938. Known as "the night of broken glass," it occurred when the Nazis went from bad to worse in a large, nation-wide pogrom. In this project, students should make a poster or memory book that describes Kristallnacht and prints up and describes at least ten of the synagogues *before* they were burned. These buildings not only were sacred but were beautiful examples of architecture that had existed for generations. Google the term *Kristallnacht* to get started. This booklet should have a title and a professional appearance.

Option I: Holocaust Memory Book

Using the Internet, create a small memory book with words and pictures of victims and their experiences *before* they went into the camps. Go to www.ushmm.org/museum/exhibit/online/phistories/ for some very moving pictures. Include a title and create a professional-looking product.

Option J: Exploring Symbols: Triangles of the Holocaust

Make a poster or other creation that shows and explains the many triangles that the Nazis used to identify their victims. Make sure to discuss why labeling people then—and now—is dangerous. Many sites on the Web describe these triangles. This poster/creation should have a title and a professional appearance.

For the Daring Student

Option K: Memorial to the Holocaust Using Geometric Shapes

Using clay, wood, metal, computer graphics, construction paper, and/or poster board, create a memorial to the Holocaust which tells a story through its shapes. Make sure the shapes that are used are symbolic of what happened. For details and pictures of other memorials around the world, go to http://fcit.coedu.usf.edu/holocaust/activity/68plan/monument.htm. This memorial should remember the victims or attempt to encourage tolerance in our world.

Option L: Student's Choice
A project option of the student's choice—please see instructor for approval. Out of respect for the victims of the Holocaust, refrain from the following:

- Diorama or Lego models of concentration camps.
- Any stick-figure drawings of *any* type.
- Any easy, "print off the Internet and paste" posters.
- Swastikas or pictures of Hitler.

5

HOW I LEARNED TO STOP WORRYING ABOUT THE TEST AND LOVE TEACHING STUDENTS TO WRITE WELL

Tricia Davis

This chapter is not so much about a big idea as it is about an intriguing idea: that spending *less* time preparing students for standardized tests may actually reap greater rewards than spending more.

A few years ago, I realized that my teaching basically revolved around the teach-review-assess and move on model of teaching, with the summative assessment pieces being largely based on New York State standardized tests. As I learned more about the writing process, I began to wonder if there was a better way of teaching and assessing through writing. Could students become more invested in their understanding of history and become better writers if I moved away from the assumption that I had to assess them in the same limited way that New York State does? And if they did, what effect might that have on their standardized test scores? The high-stakes nature of these standardized tests—for the students, the school, and me—made the idea of changing the way I was assessing a scary proposition. But then an unexpected change in my career gave me the opportunity to try.

A CHANGE BEGINS: THE TAPESTRY SCHOOL

After teaching for eight years, one at a parochial high school and seven at a traditional public high school in the suburbs, I made the move to Tapestry High School, a new urban charter high school in Buffalo, New York. I had been invited to participate in the planning of the high school piece of the Tapestry Charter, so I knew that the leadership was committed to teaching a diverse population of students, many of whom are perceived as "at risk" based on best practices research. Lynn Bass, the principal and founding administrator of the high school, cites the work of Deborah Meier, Theodore Sizer, Lisa Delpit, and other progressive reformers as the intellectual inspiration for this school.

The school already had a highly successful K–8 program which contracts with the national school reform model Expeditionary Learning Outward Bound Schools (www.elschools.org/) in its middle school. Lynn and I had researched the work of Expeditionary Learning for the secondary level, and because of its interdisciplinary, real-world learning approach with an emphasis on school culture and community, we concluded that it would be the kind of progressive small-school model on which we wanted to base the high school program. Tapestry High School was then selected by the Bill and Melinda Gates Foundation as a recipient of a grant to be used toward implementation of the Expeditionary Learning model. The many requirements the Gates Foundation has for their educational grants aligned nicely with our vision, including the requirement to serve a community of need (e.g., high poverty, low resources) and the requirement that the population of the high school not exceed 400 students (our charter was written for a total population of 300 in grades 9–12).

The first class of fifty freshmen entered Tapestry High School in September 2006. The charter calls for adding one grade per year and that each ensuing class will have seventy-five students. After five years, we will reach our capacity of 300 students. Our funding consists of a state per-pupil allowance, and our professional development is paid for by the Bill and Melinda Gates Foundation.

In many ways, I suspect this school sounds very different from the ones in which readers may be teaching. Had I been reading this chapter a few years ago, I might have stopped reading at this point, thinking that this teaching experience had little in common with my own. But let me describe some of the challenges we face at this charter school, challenges that are typical of teaching in any public urban school, and explain why I believe now that the same principles of assessing can be applied to all big idea teaching experiences.

Because of New York State charter school admission policies, Tapestry demographics must be similar to urban public schools around the country. As a result, about 50 percent of our students are African American, 15 percent are Hispanic or of mixed race, and 35 percent are European American. Typically, over 50 percent of our students come from families living in poverty; in fact, Buffalo has been recently ranked as the second poorest city in the nation. The students come from twenty-five different middle schools—public (traditional and charter), parochial, and private. Twenty percent of our students are classified as special education, primarily learning disabled, and all classrooms operate under an inclusion model. All of our students speak English as their first language or are bilingual.

New York State law requires that selection to charter schools be based on blind lottery. All applications are put in a box and selection is by a neutral third party without any prior knowledge of who has applied. There are no entrance exams and no attempt is made to directly affect the racial, economic, or gender mix.

All New York charter schools must adhere to the same state curriculum that public schools must follow, which includes the administration of a number of high-stakes standardized tests under the Regents examination program. In order to graduate, students must pass exams in mathematics, science, English language arts, global history and geography, and U.S. history and government. Charter school administrators must set goals for the percentage of students who will pass the standardized tests; if they do not reach those goals, the school may be shut down.

Our first group of students, selected by lottery, were great students with families who wanted the best for their children, but they came to us with the typical mix of challenges that many urban students face. Teaching in a charter school *is* different in some ways from teaching in a traditional public school. But in most ways, teaching history to urban students is the same no matter the kind of school context.

BIG IDEAS

I have always used big ideas to frame my own thinking and planning of the content I teach. I culled from the New York State curriculum those ideas that I thought most important and relevant and framed my units and lessons around them. For example, I framed the first unit grade 10 global history, which includes the Enlightenment and the French Revolution, around the idea that changing notions of people's relationship to their government led to revolution. With students, I expressed the big idea in the form of a question: "Why do people want to change who is in charge of their lives?" I related this question to teenagers' typical desire for more independence from their parents. Using big idea questions focused my planning and helped students to explore the causes and effects of historical events. Although my classroom activities revolved around these big ideas and guiding questions, when it came to assessing students, I felt compelled to stick to a strict regimen of Regents-based multiple-choice tests and essay prompts in order to prepare students for the high-stakes exam at the end of the course.

ASSESSING THROUGH WRITING

Prior to my move to Tapestry High School, I assessed students in a number of ways. Sometimes I used a writing assessment to take the temperature of a given class, that is, to see if students were understanding the content and able to think about it in new ways. For example, I asked students to write dinner party conversations between monarchs and philosophers where they argued for different forms of government that they would then act out, or I gave students provocative quotes from historical figures and asked the students to interpret them based on their experiences. I saw these as formative kinds of assessments, so I neither graded them nor entered them into my grade book. I did write comments back, but I used them mostly to help me decide how to proceed with any given unit.

The format of my summative assessments almost never varied, however. The writing assessments that entered my grade book were based on writing prompts that mirrored the Regents exam prompts as closely as possible. Such was the explicitly stated mandate from my public school administrators. As I recall it, my department chair said (quoting the assistant superintendent for curriculum), "All assessments must parallel New York State Regents exams." So I, along with all my colleagues in the social studies department, used state prompts like the one for the thematic essay from the June 2006 global history and geography exam (see figure 5.1). We edited the prompt to fit the content we were currently teaching and handed it out as an assignment with a due date. The expectation was that students knew how to write these essays because they had been doing them since middle school.

So in grade 10, we started the year with a unit on the Enlightenment and the French Revolution, which culminated in a document-based question (DBQ) culled from previous state exams.[1] We then moved on to the Industrial Revolution through a unit that culminated in a thematic essay such as the one mentioned above. And so my colleagues and I structured our units and assessments. Sometimes I spent a class on the writing process (e.g., brainstorming and building outlines) at the beginning of the school year, but other than that, students were on their own.

Let me take a moment here to explore some of the assumptions behind this approach to assessment:

Assumption #1: The more often a teacher asks students to practice the test format, the higher the test scores will be.
Assumption #2: Students in high school know how to write.

THEMATIC ESSAY QUESTION

Directions:

Write a well-organized essay that includes an introduction, several paragraphs addressing the task below, and a conclusion

Theme:

Conflicts between groups of people have threatened peace in many nations and regions

Task:

Identify one conflict that has threatened peace in a nation or region and

—Discuss one major cause of that conflict

—Identify two opposing groups involved in the conflict and discuss one viewpoint of each group

—Discuss the extent to which the conflict was or was not resolved

---

Figure 5.1.   Thematic Essay Question

Assumption #3: Content teachers (that is, anyone who isn't an English teacher) do not have time to teach writing.

Assumption #4: Authentic writing (almost any writing that does not involve state exam prompts) is not done in content areas.

Assumption #5: It is not important to teach students how to write except for the purpose of passing a state exam.

Ironically, there was no assumption that writing to state prompts created better historical thinkers or better writers. Frankly, social studies teachers in my experience did not talk about those things in the context of the state exams. Many of us did lots of things in our classrooms that we thought *did* make better historical thinkers, but writing around a test-based prompt was not one of them. Such writing was all about "paralleling" the exam.

Even though I was only using state prompts, I have always believed that students could learn more about historical content through the process of writing. Writing is part of the construction of knowledge to be used in conjunction with active shared learning experiences in the classroom. My students' responses to the state prompts, however, were not showing much evidence of this. In fact, their writing and thinking actually seemed to get thinner over time. Writing to state prompts seemed to result in diminishing returns. Students figured out pretty quickly the formulaic nature of the expectations.

The rubric for thematic essays on the global history and geography Regents exam has a 1–5 scale, and a score of 3 was generally agreed on by teachers that I worked with as in the 80 percent grade range. According to the rubric, a score of 3 means that the essay response "shows a satisfactory understanding of the theme or problem, addresses most aspects of the task or addresses all aspects in a limited way, and introduces the theme or problem by repeating the task and concludes by repeating the theme or problem."

Teaching students to adequately answer an essay prompt based on this rubric is not brain surgery. Teaching students to write *well* when they know that this is the standard they will be judged by seemed far more challenging. Over time, most students realized that "less *is* more" and only wrote what was absolutely necessary to get a 3. They certainly were not motivated to write well or to think historically by this scoring criteria or by essay prompts that asked them to "select a specific revolution that you have studied, and describe three factors that helped bring about that particular revolution." It's not hard to understand why students felt no investment in these kinds of prompts. The more I assigned these essays, the less and the less well students wrote! And I couldn't blame them. If they found them boring to write, I found them excruciating to read.

In retrospect, one would have thought that I could have predicted this result or, over the years, changed what I was doing to produce better results. But as they say, if you keep on doing what you're doing, you'll keep on getting what you've got. It was hard to know how to create better writers without blatantly bucking our administration mandate. Moreover, the pressure of the assumptions listed above made me feel that there really were few choices, especially since I had had little training in teaching writing. So I groped in the dark for new methods, but I never felt like anything I did in the writing process with students was especially effective. So, like the person talking to someone who doesn't understand the language, I just kept marking up students' papers and complaining even more loudly about how students could not write. Maybe, I thought, if I use a redder pen . . .

It was a shame that students could not write better, but as long as we got them through the state exam, it really didn't seem to matter. And we did get students through the state exams. Our passing rate was decent, so why worry?

But I did worry, because I couldn't shake the nagging feeling that students could and should do more. I had learned in graduate school that students could produce good writing and show their ability to think historically all at the same time that they were doing well on the state exam. And then the reality of teaching seemed to knock the ideal out of me as it does so many of us. I still believed the students could learn to write well and do well on state assessments, but not without dramatically changing the way I was doing things.

A BIG CHANGE

I was afforded that golden opportunity to change my practice in the form of a new school and new job. But I believe that most teachers could do the same thing without this kind of drastic change in situation.

The impetus for changing the way I thought about teaching writing came from expectations laid out by Tapestry High School's designation as a Delta school within the Expeditionary Learning Outward Bound (ELOB) network. A Delta (Greek for "change") school is a new high school that has been funded by the Bill and Melinda Gates Foundation in order to fully implement the ELOB model. We were one of about twenty high schools around the country with this designation. One of the expectations of a Delta high school is that literacy will be taught across the curriculum. ELOB trained all our faculty in their reading and writing workshop models. The writing workshops consist of lessons on prewriting, drafting, revising, and editing.

As mentioned above, my past writing practice consisted of a single lesson on creating an outline and then leaving students pretty much on their own. I offered extra help with their writing, but not many of my grade 10 students took me up on the offer, nor was I very confident in my ability to give them any more guidance in how to write. I hadn't had any training in teaching writing and hadn't found any useful sources for teaching writing in the social studies classroom. Frankly, as a "content" area teacher, I was intimidated by the thought of teaching students how to write. Moreover, there had been a kind of unspoken consensus among my previous colleagues that we did not have time to teach writing and it was the English teachers' jobs anyway. Oh, and by the way, shouldn't grade 10 students already know how to write?

When I changed jobs, I realized that these assumptions were not going to fly with a population of students who come from many different middle schools and backgrounds and who researchers tell us have a typical dropout rate of 50 percent. Some of my new students at Tapestry were beautiful writers, but others literally could not put two coherent sentences together on a page. The ELOB workshop, however, gave me the confidence to teach writing in a way that I hoped would meet the needs of all my students because it gave me the skills I needed to design and implement effective lessons on teaching writing in the social studies classroom. I still worried about the time issue: Global history covers 10,000 years of human history. Could I cover that content *and* teach my students to write?

With my new skills and expectations in hand, I made the decision not to assign a single state essay prompt to my freshmen. Instead, I would spend much more time on teaching them how to write.

These decisions flew in the face of some of the assumptions that I laid out earlier. I took a leap of faith and I think it has borne fruit. Once I saw students get the content through good writing, I learned to stop worrying and to love teaching students how to write. Well, okay, honestly? I still worry about the state exam. But I now see that students *can* learn how to write well and still demonstrate their knowledge of state-mandated content.

WRITING WITH RAFTS

At Tapestry, we have a commitment to teaching reading and writing across the curriculum, and Expeditionary Learning trained all of our content teachers in the writing process. We experienced the process of prewriting, conferencing, and revision that traditionally only happens in English classrooms, and we were all expected to use the process in our classrooms.

The format of the writing prompts that Expeditionary Learning favors is called RAFTS, a writing strategy developed by Nancy Vandervanter, an English teacher from the Montana Writing Project. A RAFTS writing prompt is a way of framing content so that students have to take a point of view outside of themselves while writing in an authentic genre. The acronym stands for *R*ole, *A*udience, *F*ormat, *T*opic, and *S*trong verb. The teacher writes the assignment using these five requirements. For example, in the writing workshop I took, one of the writing prompt choices was to write a speech for a public forum that one's congressional representative is attending. The purpose of the speech is to persuade the representative to continue funding or to cut funding for the Federal Theatre Project, part of the Work Progress Administration of the 1930s. The role is a constituent, the audience is the congressional representative, the format is a speech, the topic is the Federal Theatre Project, and the strong verb is "to persuade."

Almost anything would be an improvement over how I had been teaching students to write, so I was willing to give the RAFTS approach a try. And, I thought, if I'm going to do this, why not go all the way? State prompts be damned! Having left my nice tenured position, I was in a daring mood. I wouldn't ask students to write *any* state exam prompts in their freshmen year; all their writing would be in the form of RAFTS. I figured I could start their exam practice sometime in their sophomore year, since this is a two-year course with the exam at the end.

Would students be able to write better, think more effectively, *and* do well on the state exam? The students and I had a lot to lose if it didn't work. Charter schools are routinely shut down in New York for not achieving adequate state exam scores. In the back of my mind, I wondered why I wasn't content to stick with the tried and true. But frankly, the tried and true did not seem to be working in our urban school district. Test scores for the Buffalo city schools, like most large urban districts, are generally much lower than those of their suburban counterparts. The students I now taught needed something different, and our school promised to do that. I didn't see any point in holding back.

WRITING AND BIG IDEAS

The first stage in the process of developing a unit of study in the Expeditionary Learning model is developing big ideas and guiding questions, something I had been doing already though in a less formal way. One of the first writing assessments I developed was around a unit entitled "Culture Clash," which I created in collaboration with the English and living environments teachers, to examine the encounter between Europeans and Native Americans. These were the big ideas and guiding questions around which we framed the unit:

- Power can lead to dominance and oppression.
  1. How do people get power? How do people keep power?
  2. What happens when people use power?
  3. Language is potentially a source of power, oppression, and stratification.

- Values, beliefs, and cultures are interdependent.
  1. What is culture? What is civilization?
  2. What are the consequences when an individual opposes the majority?
  3. How are we to judge if the norm is sensible or moral?
- All cultures are dynamic.
  1. Where are the similarities and differences within and between cultures?
  2. How does culture change?
  3. What are the causes and effects of cultural change?

The rationale for using big ideas is that this is the content we want students to remember in ten years, not just for the exam. Big ideas reflect the state curricula but also crystallize important truths taken from social science. Guiding questions may be unanswerable or have a variety of answers, but answering them leads to the big ideas. The hope is that by focusing curricula around guiding questions and big ideas, the content taught will be more relevant and students will be more motivated to learn it.

WRITING ABOUT HISTORY WITH RAFTS

Once the big ideas are in place, assessments can be designed that address them as well as the state curriculum. I chose to assess students using the RAFTS model because of its potential to motivate students to address the big ideas and state content by getting into the heads of fictional historical figures of their own making. Let me explain the process of using RAFTS and my subsequent transitioning to state exam prompts by analyzing three sets of writing that the same group of students produced: (1) a RAFTS writing prompt students responded to at the end of their freshmen year, (2) a state exam prompt that the students turned into a RAFTS writing prompt at the beginning of their sophomore year, and (3) a state exam writing prompt that students wrote in the middle of their sophomore year. At the end of this chapter, I'll discuss what I think the implications of teaching writing this way had on my students' Regents exam results.

Having the big ideas in place and knowing the state global history curriculum well, I spent time constructing RAFTS writing tasks with the interests and needs of my students in mind. The RAFTS I wrote dealt with major elements of state curriculum, just like the Regents essay questions that I used in the past did, so I taught the same content I always had, but I intended to use a RAFTS task as the key form of assessment.

Let me begin with the state DBQ prompt on the influence of a conquering nation (see figure 5.2). Much of the content behind the

---

SAMPLE DOCUMENT-BASED QUESTION

Historical Context:

Throughout history, conquests have led to political, economic, and social changes in specific societies. Groups such as the Mongols, the Spanish, and the French have brought many changes to conquered areas.

Task:

Using information from the documents and your knowledge of global history, answer the questions that follow each document in part A. Your answers to the questions will help you write the essay in part B, in which you will be asked to:

    —Select two of the groups mentioned in the historical context

    —For each group, discuss the political, economic, and social changes that resulted from the conquest

---

Figure 5.2.   Sample Document-Based Question

2005 state essay prompt comes from unit four of the New York State curriculum, entitled "The First Global Age (1450–1770)." In order to answer the prompt, students need to know what the societies looked like before and after the conquests. According to the authors of the state curriculum, students "should understand that on the eve of the Encounter, the peoples of the Americas already had complex societies." They then specify that the content should include references to "European competition for colonies in the Americas," "the triangular trade," and "Spanish colonialism." They also pose a series of questions such as "What forces came together in the mid-1400s that made the Age of European Exploration possible?" and "What impact did European technology, food, and disease have on the Americas?" Such is the content knowledge required to adequately address the state essay prompt.

I developed my RAFTS assignment for this unit based on state curriculum content requirements and the state test prompt, but I did so in a way that I hoped would pique students' interest and motivation. For this topic, I developed a set of three writing options. The first focused on the role of a conquistador:

> You are a conquistador from Spain taking your first long journey to the New World. You've been promised great riches, but your sweetheart back in Madrid is pretty angry at you for going. Write your sweetheart a letter that will convince him/her that the journey will be worth it. Explain all the reasons that you think it is important for conquistadores to go to the New World. Also, describe some of the rumors that you have heard about the effects that the encounter has had on the civilization of the Inca who have just been conquered by your friend Fernando Pizarro.

Broken down into its RAFTS components, the assignment looks like the example shown in table 5.1.

The content that I assess in the Topic part of this prompt—"explain all the reasons that you think it is important for conquistadores to go to the New World"—fulfills the state content requirement of knowing causes of Spanish colonialism. The portion in which I ask the students to "describe some of the rumors that you have heard about the effects

Table 5.1. RAFTS Assignment—Conquistador

Role	Audience	Format	Topic	Strong Verb
Conquistador	Your sweetheart	Letter	The reasons for going to the New World and effects of Spanish conquest on the characteristics of the Inca civilization	Convince

that the encounter has had on the civilization of the Inca who have just been conquered by your friend Fernando Pizarro" is the same content as the New York State test prompt that asks for "changes that resulted from the conquest." The difference is that my assignment brought out rich, powerful writing, something that I had not experienced when my students wrote using the state essay prompts.

In response to this prompt, Rashida,[2] the most challenged special education student in my class, wrote:

> Dear sweetheart,
>   I am writing to you about my trip to the New World. I think it will be both fun and an adventure. I'm going for glory, god, and gold. . . . This is going to be expensive but I will make a lot of money. . . . I will bring you back corn and potatoes. I'm sorry that I can't bring you back a llama. Their main god [of the Inca] is the Sun God. This is a problem. I need advice to convert them to Christianity.

Where Rashida might have given up if presented with a state essay prompt, in this selection, she flourishes. Rashida hits on one of the ways that the Spanish gained power over the native cultures (conversion to Christianity) and some of the characteristics of the Inca empire (corn and potatoes, llama, sun god).

All of my special education students responded positively to the RAFTS task they selected. But so did my high-achieving students. Jamil chose the RAFTS prompt that highlighted the perspective of an Inca warrior:

> You are an Inca warrior who witnessed the capture of your emperor Atahuallpa by the Spanish. You survived the attack and want to

Table 5.2.   RAFTS Assignment—Inca Warrior

Role	Audience	Format	Topic	Strong Verb
Inca warrior	Native people of South America	Letter	The great civilization of the Incas and the advantages that the conquistadores have over the Native people	Convince

warn other native people of South America about the danger of these strange and violent white people. Write a letter which will be sent by llama throughout the region in which you explain the great civilization of the Inca and describe the Spanish conquistadores and the advantages that they have over the native people. Remember, the future of all the native people of South America depends on you convincing them of the danger!

Broken down into its component parts, the RAFTS task that Jamil responded to looks like the example shown in table 5.2.

In his response, Jamil demonstrates his knowledge of the facts, but he also captures the wonder that an Inca warrior might have felt at seeing an alien group of men:

The men who had taken us over were very strange. They wore pots on their heads, they smelt. However strange we thought they were, they had many advantages. They had these huge brown llamas [the men were riding horses] they sat on. In some way they controlled them and could slaughter us from about 5 feet above. In the hands they had a long stick of dull silver that could stab and kill us. Also they had another brown stick. They had pulled a knob and something round and small killed us. In addition a weird disease was killing us. There [were] small spots on us and [they] decimated us. None of the white men had this.

Here, Jamil certainly nails the ways in which the Spanish gained power over the Inca (horses, steel swords, guns, and disease) while quoting some of the primary sources that we read in class ("They wore pots on their heads"). In addition, I love the way he brings the

Table 5.3. RAFTS Assignment—Escaped Slave

Role	Audience	Format	Topic	Strong Verb
Escaped slave in the Americas	King or people of Mali	Letter	The characteristics of Mali culture and the reasons for Europeans capturing Africans for slavery	Warn

Inca view of the Spanish to life. He really gets into the head of the Inca warrior, demonstrating an ability to take on the perspective of a person in history. This ability to see history through the eyes of the people involved is an important skill in thinking historically.

The third RAFTS prompt I created focused on the experiences of an enslaved African:

> You are an African who has been captured and sold into slavery. When you get to the New World, you manage to escape. You want to warn your people back in Mali about the dangers of the strange white men on the coast. Write a letter that will be smuggled aboard the next slave ship going back to Africa in which you remember the wonders of Mali's civilization and explain why the white people are capturing Africans and selling them into slavery.

In this instance, the RAFTS format looks like the example shown in table 5.3.

An average-ability student, Janetta, chose this option. Like Jamil, she finds a way to build a plausible narrative around the factual information we discussed in class:

> These people with no skin tried to catch me but I was too fast for them then some of our own people came and got me. Then they dragged me to this huge boat, and people from different kinds of villages were there but none spoke our languages so I could not talk to anyone. As they put us on the boat I started to think about Mali. All of the gold we had, we were a rich country. . . . We had one of the strongest armies. . . . I love being a Muslim and the mosques that are in Mali are so pretty I haven't seen any other building so pretty. . . . Those were the good days. But now all I can do is just remember things.

Janetta alludes to the difficult subject of African collusion in the slave trade ("some of our own people") and makes clear the fact that slavers intentionally mixed African people on the boats so they could not communicate ("so I could not talk to anyone"). She also describes some of the characteristics of the Mali civilization (gold, army, Muslim, mosques), but in a way she would never have been allowed or encouraged to do on a Regents exam essay.

I am most gratified by these writing responses when students' voices come through like this. It reflects an ownership and an investment that I do not believe my students ever experienced when I assigned Regents essays. And as an added bonus, these responses are a treat to read! Each piece is unique; they are never formulaic. They make me laugh, they make me sad, as I feel the persona the student has adopted behind the writing.

CHALLENGES OF STUDENT WRITING

The task of letter writing is, of course, somewhat artificial, as one cannot assume that an Inca warrior, an escaped slave, or a Spanish conquistador would be literate. My RAFTS tasks, therefore, may not be seen as an "authentic" assessment in the way that observers like Grant Wiggins (Wiggins, 1993) might expect. But the ability of my students to bring a real sense of historical perspective *and* the humanity of historical actors is clear. I have never experienced this kind of writing to a state prompt.

As I look back through the students' work and my own comments on it, however, I see a danger in this kind of writing that would never be a problem on a state essay. Some of the students got so involved in the emotional expression of their writing that they forgot to respond to the question. This omission occurred most often among the students who wrote as the escaped slave. We spent a lot of time in class on the horrors of the Middle Passage, and some students just ran with that. For example, Maureen went on and on about the conditions on the boat:

They brought more of my people on board. People were struggling trying to get away. The more they tried to wiggle out of the metal circles [shackles] the tighter they got around the neck. . . . Everyone thought that the skeletons [white people] were going to eat us. . . . We were put in the bottom of the boat and our feet were locked together. We were very smooshed and the smell was horrible.

Maureen wrote three pages of graphic descriptions like this in which she often used material from primary sources we read in class. Unfortunately, she did not get around to addressing the content of the prompt. At the end of her essay, I wrote, "Great writing, Maureen, but you did not address the content of the prompt! Why were Africans being enslaved <u>and</u> what was the civilization of Mali like? Rewrite, please." I find it funny and ironic that the means by which I was trying to motivate students turned out to be the downfall of some. This girl certainly was motivated to write a sophisticated response, but she completely missed the practical point of the essay.

Another student, Alyssa, also focused her piece on the experiences of the escaped slave and missed the bigger question:

They led us to a boat and inside the boat were cramped spaces laying side by side hardly breathing. Not knowing what was coming many people refused to eat and jumped off the boat taking their lives. Where you lay you may end up next to a dead person and unkindly foul smells I never encountered in my life. Many men on the boat rebelled and sacrifice their lives for freedom.

Like Maureen, Alyssa really explores the horrors that enslaved Africans endured, but she fails to address the content of the prompt. I wrote, "Alyssa, you need more detail on <u>why</u> Africans were enslaved <u>and</u> the culture of Mali. Rewrite, please." I can see my frustration in the dark underlines I put under some of my words.

I love that my students were engaged in the topic, but the question remained: "How do I get students to think beyond the emotional and compelling events in history and explore the causes and effects of these events?"

A related problem was that students did not always address all parts of the writing prompt. This challenge also appeared in students' responses to state writing prompts. Since the Regents essays often have more than one part, I believed it was important to construct prompts that asked students to write about more than one aspect of the content. Often students explained one part of the prompt with good, historically accurate details but then forgot to write about the other part. At the end of Sabrina's essay describing a conquistador perspective, I wrote, "Good job on the reason for going, but you need to add content about the effects on the Inca." To Bethany, I commented, "Nice job on descriptions of Mali. Add something more about <u>why</u> whites started using Africans as slaves." So the problem students had in responding to all aspects of the state prompts carried over into my RAFTS assignments.

I believe now that the reason none of my attempts at teaching students the writing process were effective in the past, in part at least, was because the Regents essay questions failed to motivate my students. Using the RAFTS approach, I started to see that students felt an investment in their writing that they had not experienced before. This investment, as well as my own clearer vision of how to teach students to write, resulted in a consistent improvement in students' writing over the course of the school year. Students who previously had written very little were now writing more. More importantly, they used more and more accurate content to tell their stories. Students who were decent writers at the beginning of the school year wrote compelling narratives with strong content by the end of the school year. Students' writing and content knowledge improved, largely it seemed, when writing prompts were used that they cared about. The nature of the task, then, seemed to bring out good writing, writing that was rich in content and emotionally powerful.

As noted above, however, the strength of this kind of task did not solve all the writing problems that students face. A few just could not get beyond the emotion of their writing to fully understand and respond to the task in front of them. Ironically, addressing only some parts of the writing task is sufficient for state policymakers:

students score a 3 on the state exam if they "address most of the task." Yet as my students increasingly demonstrated their content and rhetorical competence, my expectations of them grew and eventually eclipsed those of the state exam writers. In a sense, then, the more I moved *away* from the state test prompts, the more I moved *toward* the kinds of assessments that mirrored my teaching goals.

THE OTHER "R": REVISION

The challenges notwithstanding, my students were really demonstrating their knowledge of the history content by writing to RAFTS prompts. However, it wasn't just the RAFTS that contributed to my students' writing success. Through my training with Expeditionary Learning, I became committed to another layer of writing instruction: revision.

Like many teachers, I once graded students' writing, handed it back, and neither they nor I ever looked at it again. I told students that I would accept revisions, but I never taught them how to do that, nor did my grading system support the idea. If I gave students a passing grade (65 or above), most were not interested enough in the assignment to revise it—after all, they had passed. If I did not give a student a passing grade, she or he was probably not motivated or skilled enough in the first place to bother with revising. Although their lack of response discouraged and puzzled me, I was not sure what to do about it, so I chugged along with my curriculum, ignoring the fact that students were not becoming better writers.

As I learned more about teaching writing with Expeditionary Learning, I realized that writing is a process and that good writing requires revision. Using the writer's workshop model, I taught the process of writing. I took the time to teach prewriting, drafting, and revising. For major writing assignments, my students did peer reviews and one-on-one revision conferences with me. The feedback they got from each other helped sustain interest in the assignment, and the individual attention I gave to each student helped them develop a sense of the importance of their writing. In addition, another

ELOB structure encouraged revision—mastery grading. We use a 1–4 grading system, with 3 being a passing grade. The expectation is that students will revise and remediate all assignments until they have reached a 3. We have a variety of structures in place to support that practice, including separate literacy classes and mandatory after-school help, and students come to see it as the norm, albeit an annoying but ultimately rewarding norm. Now when I hand back a paper that asks for a revision, most of the time I get it. I have taught my students how to revise, and they know that we, as a school faculty, support them getting it done. Students may not enthusiastically embrace the idea, but by the time they are sophomores, they understand that revision is part of the learning process.

THE TRANSITION: FROM RAFTS TO STATE PROMPTS AND BACK AGAIN

I was fortunate to have the same group of students back for their sophomore year in the global history and geography course. This is an unusual situation. In my last teaching position, I may have taught some of the same students for both years of the course sequence, but it was more a matter of scheduling than intent. Continuing with the same group of students is a real bonus: As their teacher, I knew exactly where each student was in terms of her or his skills and content knowledge development—who was flying, who was still struggling, and everyone in between. Moreover, I had evidence of some very good writing from almost all of them during their freshmen year, so I knew I could jump off from there.

That said, I struggled with competing concerns: I thought students should start seeing what the Regents writing prompts looked like early in their sophomore year, but I did not want to fall into the trap of creating parallel assessments. If I simply started using state writing prompts as my assessments, I feared that I would lose the motivation and interest that I saw students gain in their freshmen year. My experience told me that writing to state prompts was a sure-fire way of turning students off. However, I thought students should start becoming familiar with the Regents format. Moreover, I wanted to assure them that they had been writing about the state curriculum throughout their freshmen year even though they had not seen a single state prompt.

So I decided to create a transition whereby students themselves (instead of me) took a state essay prompt and turned it into a RAFTS prompt. The assignment looked like the example shown in figure 5.3.

What I thought was a simple and straightforward task, turning a state prompt into a RAFTS task, totally boggled most of my students' minds. They did not see that what they had been writing in the form of RAFTS was really just a version of a state exam prompt, and I had not made that connection explicit to them. Instead of the independent, confident writers I knew them to be, my students turned into a room full of hands in the air and a din of whining for my help!

At that point, I realized that I needed to model what I expected them to do. After the first disastrous class period, I made transparencies of several Regents prompts that addressed the Encounter topic and put them side by side with the RAFTS task I had developed and they had written. During the next class, I did a think-aloud in which I explained my process of turning the state prompt into a RAFTS assignment, and we discussed where they saw similarities and differences between the two.

No surprise, this approach went much better. Most students now saw how they could transform the state prompt on the Industrial Revolution into a RAFTS task. For example, the first choice became:

> You are a child working in a textile factory in Manchester, 1845. You are writing a diary entry in which you describe your working and living conditions. You also express your hope that things will get better because of the work of unions and Parliament.

Once they got rolling, some students decided to write as different roles than the choices I had given them. For example, one chose to write as a journalist researching the conditions of industrialization.

GLOBAL HISTORY AND GEOGRAPHY
Creating a RAFTS Writing Invitation

Below is a typical Regents exam essay prompt. You will create your own RAFTS writing invitation based on this essay prompt.

Historical Context: During the Industrial Revolution, 1750–1914, the creation of new inventions, the development of the factory system, and the expansion of business resulted in many changes in our economic lives. Industrialization changed the way goods were made, but it also changed the politics and society of the modern world.

Task: In a well-organized essay, describe some of the negative results of the Industrial Revolution. These may include working systems, working conditions, child labor, and/or living conditions in the city. Also, explain how these negative conditions were addressed in the nineteenth century. Your explanation may include economic theories, labor unions, reform laws, and/or women activists.

Your first assignment is to turn this into a RAFTS writing invitation. Here are the choices:

ROLE	AUDIENCE	FORMAT	TOPIC	STRONG VERB
Child in 1845	Yourself	Diary	See above	You decide!
Union organizer	Fellow workers	Speech	See above	You decide!
Member of Parliament	Other members	Speech	See above	You decide!
Factory owner	Readers of the London Times	Letter	See above	You decide!

The first thing you need to do is write out the RAFTS invitation here:

Figure 5.3.   Creating a RAFTS Writing Invitation

My point in this conversion exercise was twofold. First, I wanted to expose students to the language and format of the Regents exam essay prompts. Second, I hoped to show them that they had, in fact, been writing about the state curriculum content all along, even though they had not addressed a single state prompt.

Much of the writing that emerged once the students had created their own RAFTS assignments was powerful and convincing. For example, Janine wrote as a child working in the mines:

> I move all the carts in the mines up and out of the mines when it's in little spaces and men can't fit. Where I work is very dirty. I have asthma and it gets worse every time . . . it's very dangerous. Just yesterday one of the children who worked with me was pushing the cart full of coal up the rail and a whole bunch of rocks fell on him and he died.

Not only does Janine paint a really nice visual of this child's life, but she made a real-world connection to her own: She has asthma.

Linda also wrote as a child laborer, but she captured the dynamic and uncertain quality of the laborers' existence:

> You'll never believe what happened! Ok, so I got to work and there's this huge crowd of people standing outside the factory so I start pushing through the crowd to get to the gates so I can go start my work and not get in trouble. All around me people were yelling about how cruel the factory is and that children shouldn't be forced to work here under these conditions, women should have the same pay as men . . . so lots of people go together and went on something called "strike" until the factory owner gives them what they want.

In this passage, I love the way that Linda lets us know that she is just an uninformed child by putting the word strike in quotes while, at the same time, making it clear that she knows the goal of a worker's strike. In another part of her response, she says that "we even started something called a union" and her father explains to her what that means. Linda uses devices of voice and narrative to show us that she is thinking like a child, but she uses those same devices to show us that she knows the content.

As they did with the RAFTS on the slave trade, some students who wrote as child laborers got wrapped up in the emotional content of their writing and ignored the major components of the task. In her first draft, Priscilla spent three pages describing her working conditions, the poor pay, dangerous machines, and her family's suffering, but she failed to describe how conditions changed. In her second draft, she alluded to the need for people to change the condition—"I want someone to step up and fix the gap between our bosses and the workers. Someone needs to speak up for the rights of us and the job done"—but she still did not get to the specifics of union unrest or legislative reform.

The challenge of getting all my students to see the whole picture of the task carried over into their sophomore year. Moreover, the ones who did address the whole task lapsed at times into a very dry and uninspired prose. They wrote lists of facts about laws passed to address the conditions of the Industrial Revolution without any real sense of voice that they demonstrated when describing the conditions themselves. For example, Bethany offered a factually correct but very detached narrative:

> The skilled worker led the way for the unions cause . . . and gave them extra bargaining power. . . . The women also formed unions. Then in the United States and Britain the women started to wonder why their rights were being denied. The Industrial Revolution proved a mixed blessing for women.

I wrote in response, "This all sounds a little too textbooky!" Clearly this part of industrialization did not resonate with students nearly as much as the horrors of child labor.

WRITING TO THE STATE PROMPT: THE GOOD, THE BAD, AND THE UGLY

Midway through the first trimester, I felt compelled to have my now sophomore students directly address a Regents exam writing prompt. I was anxious about getting them ready for the state test and I wanted to see if they could transfer their good experiences with writing about history to an exam situation. I decided to use a document-based question that was originally piloted by the state when the curriculum and exam were changed in 2000. The topic was the positive and negative effects of imperialism. The task included eight documents that students needed to use in addition to their background knowledge when addressing the prompt:

> *Historical Context*: Imperialism has been interpreted from a variety of viewpoints. The documents below express various viewpoints about the positive and negative effects of imperialism.
> *Task*: Evaluate both the positive and negative effects of imperialism.

My students' responses were generally good; they would have received at least a 3 had this really been a state exam. They fulfilled the requirements of the state rubric adequately. Breaking down the population of students, I found that 92 percent of the general education students (students without disabilities) scored a 3 or higher, a passing rate comparable to their suburban counterparts. The group that did not seem to show great gains was the special education students. Only about 13 percent of these students scored a 3 and none scored any higher than a 3.

Several months later, these same students took the actual Regents exam in global history and geography. The results largely paralleled those around the imperialism essay earlier in the year, with 95 percent of the general education students passing the exam. Many more of my special education students passed the exam (i.e., 38 percent) than is typical in inclusive classrooms, but I was left with mixed feelings. I was thrilled that so many of my students had passed, but some big concerns remained.

CONCLUSION

It seems clear to me that, by many measures, my commitment to teaching the writing process and using RAFTS assignments really paid off. Most students evinced an enjoyment of writing about history through the voices of historical people, they demonstrated their knowledge of the content, and they performed well on the high-stakes New York State exam. It is equally clear to me, however, that the needs of my special education students require more attention. Although our special education teachers make sure that we are fulfilling the legal requirements of these students' Individual Education Plans, we need to think carefully about why these students are not seeing the same gains as their general education peers and what we can do about it.

In the end, my conviction that students could do well on state exams without endless test prep has been borne out. They learned to write well (at least most of the time) and I really enjoyed their writing. I still worry about the state exam and will probably never give up some form of test preparation. Given the statistics for most inner-city schools, we simply do not have the luxury of not thinking about these tests. But reaching beyond these exams has made me a better teacher and my students better writers and thinkers.

NOTES

1. The document-based question (DBQ) is an essay prompt that requires the use of a number of historical documents provided in order to support the thesis.

2. I have changed the students' names but maintained most of their original writing. Ellipses indicate where I have removed some words for clarity's sake. Brackets indicate where I have added an explanatory note.

REFERENCE

Wiggins, G. (1993). Assessment: Authenticity, context, and validity. *Phi Delta Kappan, 75*(3), 200–214.

6

BIG EXPECTATIONS: BIG IDEAS IN HONORS AND INCLUSION CLASSES

Sarah Foels

When I entered grade 8 as a child on the verge of young adulthood, I did not like social studies. I did not hate it either. In fact, my parents had already taken me on various adventures throughout the United States as well as to Mexico and France. By the age of twelve, I had seen the Empire State Building, the Golden Gate Bridge, the Smithsonian Museum, the Mayan ruins at Chichen Itza, and the Palace of Versailles. I felt fortunate to have visited these historic places, but social studies in school seemed very different from these personal experiences. I could not reach out and touch what I read in a textbook. It was not motivating to simply read and memorize facts about the past. And, as far as I was concerned, it was a subject area that took a considerable amount of time to study and that did not have any immediate relevance to my life. Science and math were much more practical and easier for me to grasp. Besides, what did the past have to do with me?

But then I had a social studies teacher who brought the past to life and made me understand how to be an effective teacher. We memorized and took the Oath of Office, created our own govern-ments and currency systems, negotiated as a union with employers for a better contract, and pretended to be news reporters on the *Maine* incident. Our unit on World War I involved a mock participa-tion in trench warfare. This was not the type of social studies class to which I was accustomed. The teacher made us want to work both inside and outside of class. I did well and I wanted to know more about the past. And so began my love for social studies and my in-terest in teaching.

I continued to take more social studies classes in high school. In college, I majored in history and adolescence education. I found a love for a subject area at a young age and could not resist learn-ing more about it. I took trips to England, Arizona, Quebec, South Carolina, and various historic sites around New York State. I rented and watched historic movies and movies based on historic events. I even wrote some short historical fiction stories based on what I was learning in my history classes. I was obsessed and I could not let go. I promised myself that I would never forget what a great inspiration my social studies teachers had been to me and how they had helped to shape the course of my life. Student teaching gave me my first opportunity to experiment with different teaching philosophies and share my love for social studies with young minds.

And, initially, I did not forget. Having learned about constructiv-ism and collective learning experiences in my college education classes, I enthusiastically applied these theories during my student teaching placements. I created a lesson for Advanced Placement (AP) U.S. government classes at my high school placement that allowed students to work in groups to debate their positions about their views of lobbying and interest groups. I was amazed by the maturity and the detail with which these students executed their arguments. What began as simply a lesson on lobbying turned into a basis for a larger discussion of the existence and effectiveness of interest groups. By the end of the unit, students seemed to feel con-fident in their social studies skills as well as comfortable with using the terminology and ideas associated with the main topic. I blended this style of teaching with lecture and discussion in order to delve into other key ideas of the AP U.S. government curriculum.

Later, at my middle school placement, I developed an activity for grade 7 classes that allowed my students to analyze the extent to which Lewis and Clark accomplished the goals set forth by President Jefferson. Looking at primary and secondary documents, students worked in cooperative learning groups to determine the goals of the mission and then to rate Lewis and Clark in their effectiveness in achieving these goals. The students were able not only to determine the goals of the mission but also to support their rating score for Lewis and Clark with specific, logical reasons. When groups did not agree on the score, we tried to account for these discrepancies and determined an overall class rating for the explorers based on group ratings. The students seemed to enjoy participating in this historical analysis and were very competitive in defending their answers. I was pleased that twelve-year-olds could be so reflective and creative with social studies, but I was not completely surprised. Somehow, I had the feeling that they were capable of the work and perhaps had not been given many opportunities to be actively involved in the process of learning.

After completing my undergraduate degree, I felt that I was ready to begin my career as a teacher. I knew that I had a strong pedagogical background and was well versed in the discipline of social studies, but I also recognized my lack of experience in the classroom and understood that there was considerable room for growth in my teaching practices. I was nervous and excited about showcasing my ideas for different students and learning environments. In an era of assessment-driven learning, I was afraid that my constructivist philosophy would seem idealistic and impractical. However, I hoped that the school at which I worked would accept me and view my teaching style as an asset rather than a drawback.

After several interviews, I found the perfect match. I received a position as a grade 8 social studies teacher at Depew Middle School. During my first year, I was assigned to teach the second half of a two-year course on U.S. history to four regular education classes and one honors class. I was enthusiastic about working with the school's curriculum and hoped to be able to bring lessons to my students that would keep them engaged and make social studies meaningful for them. I was ready to embark on my first experiment in full-time teaching.

THE SCHOOL ENVIRONMENT

The Depew Union Free School District is located in a small, suburban village near Buffalo, New York. There are fewer than 2,500 students in the entire district, 96 percent of which are white. Only a few students are of African American or Asian American background. Despite the lack of racial diversity in the village, the socioeconomic levels of the families are quite varied. For example, about 20 percent of the students in the district are eligible for a free lunch. There is no class tension visible in the school, but the mix of blue-collar and white-collar community members becomes quite clear as students begin to talk about what their parents do for a living and what supplies they can afford for the school year. From my experiences, I have gladly noticed that there is no correlation between socioeconomic class and academic success. With the help of the caring teachers in this district, students who want to work hard and are willing to learn will do so under any circumstance.

As far as academics are concerned, the school performs at a comparable level within the range of similar schools in the area. Most students receive proficient scores, though reading and writing tasks sometimes prove difficult for students at the grade 8 level. Nevertheless, the district has the financial resources to invest in programs to continue improving upon these scores. Also, there is great administrative encouragement for purchasing new technology, including the Classroom Performance System student response pads, Smart Boards, laptop carts, and various Internet programs that allow for the creation of wikis and blogs. Furthermore, since the average class size is about twenty students, children have an opportunity to work closely with their peers and teachers. There is no concern about having too many students in one class or about individual students being neglected because of large class sizes. Finally, as the teachers in Depew are relatively young, with an average level of experience at twelve years, the staff welcomes and encourages the use of current teaching practices.

Most importantly, the district is extremely supportive of the academic freedom of its teachers. There is even a clause in the union contract that protects each teacher's right to make final decisions on grading policies, formative and summative assessments, and implementation of a variety of pedagogical methods. Our teachers are treated as professionals and are allowed to make informed decisions based on student interests and needs. Curriculum maps and guides have been developed and are utilized, but teachers are free to structure unit and lesson plans as they desire. And while the middle school and district administrators place an emphasis on improving state test scores in the intermediate-level core subject areas, they are not driven by these numbers alone. The social development of students is considered equally as important as their academic development. According to the school mission statement, the school "will stress the development of the whole child by instilling in students a sense of positive self-worth, self-respect, and self-confidence and a belief that each can succeed. Depew Middle School, in cooperation with families, will provide students with the necessary academic and personal/social knowledge, skills, and attitudes to succeed in the middle-level grades, high school, and beyond."

Basically, Depew Middle School is a teacher's dream school. The classroom is a place where teachers can utilize different pedagogical practices and help students to develop the academic and social skills necessary for success in high school. While there are formal evaluations throughout the year connected to standards and the content, as long as teachers show that what they are doing is related to clear goals and is meaningful for students, no one questions their professional judgment. There is a great sense of respect for teachers in Depew, which I think is probably not found in most districts today.

Administrators, parents, and community members regard teachers as important and intelligent members of society responsible for shaping the lives of their children.

THE EXPERIMENT

During my first year of teaching, I wanted to apply everything that I had learned in college. I was not confident that my regular education students would be capable of handling the work, so I began my experiments with constructivism in my honors class. There were only twelve students in the honors class, and they seemed bright and energetic. I decided if the lessons were successful at the honors level, then I would modify them for the remaining four classes and analyze the results. I believed that I could eventually bring the regular education classes up to the level of the honors students and push the honors students to work with even more complex and detailed concepts. Having worked with AP students before, I had high expectations for my own students.

Beginning with a unit on the causes of the Civil War, I started to get a feel for how much experience students had with being actively involved in their learning process. In one of my first lessons, I found documents pertaining to difficult opinions on the issue of slavery and asked the students to determine the pros and cons of slavery. At first, the honors students did not know what to do. They were not having difficulty reading or understanding the documents. They just did not know why there were different perspectives on the issue. They believed that slavery was wrong and had a hard time finding a reasonable explanation for someone to support it. They did not understand how someone could justify the existence of such a terrible institution. As I had planned the lesson for only a forty-minute period and the class was still working on document analyses, I began asking questions to refocus them and get them to see the issue from the perspective of a slave or slave owner. Most students were still acting confused. By the end of the period, everyone was frustrated, including me. I simply could not comprehend what went wrong. The students appeared to be smart enough to interpret the documents, but they were having trouble understanding the historical context in which the documents were written.

That evening, I spent some time further reflecting on my honors lesson. As I thought about it more, I realized that I had spent so much time focusing on the activity that I had not clearly stated the goals and objectives of the lesson. Also, I had not taken into account their personal experiences and the extent to which grade 8 students think about the world in terms of themselves. This is not to say that my students were self-centered, but that I had not given them any means by which to connect to the past. This was not a government or economics class that I could easily relate to today's world. It was U.S. history and not recent at all. They needed me to do something to better help them reach out to the past.

It was then that I began thinking about one of the methods courses I had taken in college. I remembered the professor teaching about the GAP method of creating lesson plans. This involved thinking of the goal (G) of the lesson first before the assessment (A) and plan of action (P). The goal had to be general enough to encompass the subject area content as well as the significance of the lesson. I had automatically written my honors lesson plan this way, but I realized that I had forgotten the main point of the GAP system of lesson design: to make sure that all parts of the lesson are focused on the goal. I must have been so excited to try out the activity that I had not made the goal clear to my students. They were fumbling through the document analysis not only because they had no idea why they were doing it but also because they could not see why it was important to understand the concept of perspective in studying history.

Before class the next day, I redesigned the lesson to focus on a specific goal. I wanted the honors students to consider both sides of the argument on slavery and I decided that the lesson goal would be to determine whether or not slavery was a necessary evil during the antebellum period. This would allow me to draw upon their perception of slavery as an evil institution but also help them consider that slavery might have been viewed as necessary or even helpful to some people in the past. However, I decided that students would have an easier time connecting to the overarching goal of the lesson if I first posed the following personal questions at the beginning of class: "Think of an argument that you had with someone. What reasons did you give to support your ideas? What reasons did he or she give to support his or her ideas? Who was 'right' and who was 'wrong'? Explain." I had my students write their answers for a few minutes and then asked them to share their responses with the class.

Almost everyone raised their hand and talked about their experiences with parents, friends, and relatives. Most agreed that each side of the argument in which they were involved had legitimate concerns but that it was difficult to reach an agreement because each person wanted his or her own needs to be met. As a result, the majority of students said that neither side was completely right or wrong—they just had different perspectives and therefore different opinions. This discussion also brought up the ideas of compromise and appeasement, which we would be addressing quite soon as we moved closer to the unit on the Civil War. I suddenly felt much better about trying the document task again, with some slight modifications. It seemed as though my students were beginning to see that perspectives on an issue changed depending on the individual person.

After this ten-minute task, I brought out the documents from the previous day and asked students to move into their groups. I explained that they needed to categorize the documents into those that supported slavery and those that opposed it. I then wrote the following question of the lesson on the board: "Was slavery a necessary evil or just plain evil?" We discussed the meaning of the phrase "necessary evil" and I explained the next activity for the lesson. I wanted students to draw a T-chart on the group white board, with one side labeled "necessary evil" and the other side labeled "plain evil." They would use information from the documents to fill out specific ideas that supported each point of view on the issue of slavery. When they were finished with this task, the group then needed to come to a decision about their answer to the question and be able to explain their choice using specific examples.

Walking around, I saw that the more focused GAP plan had worked. With a clear goal in mind and a little more guidance in analyzing the documents, the groups were hurriedly jotting down details from the documents in the appropriate columns of the T-chart. When I asked students to individually explain why these ideas fit under each category, they could give me specific reasons and relate it back to the person who had written the document. At the end of class, each group shared its findings and gave an answer to the lesson's question. Many groups chose to say that it was perceived as a necessary evil for those who owned slaves or who had a positive experience as slaves, but that it appeared to be just plain evil to those who had negative experiences as slaves or who had witnessed the cruel treatment of slaves. Since I did not support any particular answer to the question, I placed value on the students' judgment and reasoning. As long as their ideas were clear and could be backed up with evidence from the documents, I did not feel the need to intervene in the presentation of their group's findings.

Though I did not realize it at the time, I had stumbled upon the world of "big ideas" for lesson planning. Instead of focusing exclusively on the teaching of content, I had attempted to find a broader question or idea that students could connect with. By asking students to relate arguments in general to analyzing the validity of different historical arguments with respect to a specific topic, I had been able to make the content meaningful and open to evaluation. It seemed that the students had enjoyed answering an open question about the topic instead of simply memorizing and regurgitating information. I had not told them what to think but had given them ownership over their own knowledge and comprehension of the material.

Throughout the rest of the year, I made sure to include activities that were focused on "big ideas" or that placed students in a historical situation. These were interspersed with more traditional methods of teaching in order to pace the delivery of the content. I kept the history in chronological order but created individual lessons that centered around general themes. When learning about late nineteenth-century immigration, students were asked to analyze the positive and negative experiences of different immigrant groups that came into America as well as examine nativist attitudes within the United States toward immigrants. Once again, this required students to challenge notions of "right" or "wrong" perspectives in history through a big idea: "Was immigration positive or negative? For whom? Why?" To teach about the nature of and the fight for civil rights, I asked students to research and assume the personas of different leaders in civil rights movements of the twentieth century. This included African Americans, Hispanics, and women. We had a round-table discussion on the value of basic citizens' rights and the means by which citizens can best maintain and defend their rights. This taught students not only to examine the importance of civil rights in terms of their own lives but also to consider the best ways to communicate with and gain support in the fight for change.

When I taught about the First World War, I created a unit based on a big idea: "Was the First World War worth fighting for?" During the unit, I had students participate in mock trench warfare, research the pros and cons of the new weapons used during the war, and study the statistics of the war in terms of damages and deaths. In the end, we were able to discuss whether or not the First World War was worth fighting from several perspectives. I liked how the honors students reacted to these lessons, and as a result, I modified them and implemented them in the regular education classes at a more basic level during the year.

There was a little bit of resistance at first because the regular education students did not know how to approach the big ideas. When I asked them to consider broader analyses of topics in discussions and essays, they thought that I was looking for specific answers and kept asking me whether or not they had the correct answers. In a unit on the civil rights movement, I remembered trying to teach the concept of civil rights to students using Supreme Court cases related to student rights in schools as examples. I was surprised to find that students had no concept of their own rights in school, but they seemed to enjoy reading about and reenacting parts of the cases. When I prompted them to explain whether or not children actually have civil rights, the students were silent. I knew from the lesson that they understood the concept of civil rights and had plenty of examples to reference. Someone finally raised a hand and asked, "So, what's the right answer?" I was horrified. I questioned whether or not I had just wasted forty minutes of class time. I tried to rephrase the prompt, adding that students could use examples learned in class to explain *their thoughts* on the subject. Some brave students volunteered their ideas and I simply listened, occasionally asking for them to justify their responses. Once my students saw that I was not belittling them or correcting their explanations, more raised their hands and shared their answers. It was not exactly what I was looking for, but it was a start. At least the students knew that I valued their ideas and that they could express their thoughts in a safe environment.

After experiencing a few lessons centered on big ideas, they began to realize that they would need to be able to determine the answers on their own and use details to support their answer. I was able to begin assigning regular journal entries based on the big ideas learned in class. Throughout station and cooperative learning activities, students even began to develop their own big ideas about the documents and ideas presented in class. They began to understand the concepts of personal perspective and historical context. I felt comfortable challenging these students, and I discovered that they had some interesting ideas to share.

During a lesson on the changing culture during the 1920s, with a focus on the question of whether or not there was a "return to normalcy" after the First World War, one student made a connection between the past and the present without my prompting. She said that the new fashions, music, and literature must have been shocking to previous generations, just like the trends of today often make parents and grandparents feel that the "good old days" are gone. The thought had crossed my mind, but I did not think to emphasize it in the lesson because perhaps the students had not experienced this. Every year when I teach that unit, I make sure to generate a question or two to help students relate to the Roaring Twenties.

By the end of the year, I was happy with what I had accomplished both in the honors and regular education classes. The students seemed to retain information well, though they still had a bit of trouble keeping events in chronological order, and were good at explaining and writing about historical documents. They had a voice in what they were learning and they were proud of it. My experiment had not been perfect, but it had generally worked and made me confident that I could continue to improve on my lesson plans for future years. Then I found out in June that I would be switching from the honors team to the inclusion team. This was done for several reasons, none of which involved anything that I had done or failed to do. The switch made me not only nervous, as I had never taught special education students before, but also hesitant to continue on the path that I had started. I did not know the capabilities of these students. With this unexpected change, I began to abandon what I had accomplished over the past year and forgot about the progress I had made teaching with big ideas.

THE PRESSURE IS ON

When I first switched from teaching my small class of honors students to teaching an inclusion class with twice as many students and a consultant teacher during my second year, I was convinced that my use of big ideas and hands-on activities would no longer be feasible on such a frequent basis. How were students with disabilities going to handle generalizations and abstract ideas? How was I going to manage such a big class and still accomplish what I had tried out the year before? I naively believed that they would only be able to grasp the content to some extent and would struggle thinking deeply about it.

Since the set of students this year were academically low, and generally lacked confidence with skills in social studies, I felt less confident about my teaching methods. The big ideas caused a great deal of confusion and resistance for some classes. There was only one class that consistently performed well with these, and I was able to continue expanding my pedagogical practices with them. With only the safe haven of my self-proclaimed "honors" group, I became frustrated and started to panic about the intermediate social studies assessment. After seeing that it was taking the majority of my students a longer time to process and remember social studies concepts, I discarded many of the big ideas that I had created my first year and started to focus on covering the content.

This did not mean that I rejected my activities and ideas from the previous year, but that I did not use them as often in developing and implementing lessons. There were still lessons that involved role-playing and connections between the past and the present, but not as many as the amount that I had experimented with months before. And they were not necessarily connected to big ideas; they were sometimes more about the activity itself than the overarching theme of the lesson or unit. In the process, I became consumed with the fear of teaching all of the material covered on the assessment. My expectations lowered for my students, and with it, my confidence in my teaching practices declined as well. The kids still learned a great deal about U.S. history, but they had not experienced history the way I had wanted them to. I had given them breadth, not depth, of material.

By the end of the year, I was exhausted and somewhat disillusioned. What had happened to me and all that I had once supported in education? Would all of my future classes be this academically challenging? Would this obsession with standardized testing and school assessment ever go away? When was I going to be able to teach again like I did before? Little did I realize that help was just around the corner—in the form of a graduate studies class at Buffalo State College. In pursuit of my master's degree, I found the motivation to come back to big ideas again.

THE EPIPHANY

During the fall semester of 2007, I began a required graduate course in social studies education entitled Teaching Social Studies. The professor seemed very enthusiastic and open to current ideas about pedagogy. After the first few meetings, I began to see that her support of constructivist teaching and the importance of emphasizing

multiple perspectives coincided with my classroom ideals. I particularly liked the prologue reading on *The Strange Death of Silas Deane*
and our discussion about the Jacksonian Era. In the former reading,
authors Davidson and Lytle (2000) presented a complex historical
case to show just how subjective history can be. They showed that
historians may never know exactly how Silas Deane died because
they only have personal documents from which to select and
analyze. These documents could be exaggerated, incorrect, or just a
matter of opinion. As a teacher, I had always wanted to emphasize
that history could only be an approximation of multiple perspectives, not an exact truth. Until I read this article, I had forgotten
how important this idea was to me and to my teaching philosophy.
I began to think that a modified version of this story could serve as
the basis of discussion for a few lessons, but then I wondered just
how much time I would "waste" with an activity that had little to
do with the state test. I was uncertain about whether my students
would even understand what I was trying to accomplish.

Similarly, our class discussion on the Jacksonian Era opened my
eyes to a new way of constructing a unit, but I was hesitant to implement the practice. After the class read several conflicting articles
on Andrew Jackson, the professor had us consider the persona of
the "real" Andrew Jackson. Was he a hero who had made important
decisions during the War of 1812 and who, as president, worked
hard to champion egalitarianism? Or was he a villain who tried to
manipulate the system to get his way and who destroyed the lives
of Native Americans? It was hard to come to a consensus because
each reading showed a different side of Jackson and emphasized
unique qualities about him. The most confusing part was that they
were all historically sound pieces of research. I thought that the
theme of "hero or villain" sounded like a great idea for a unit because there were no correct views on the issue. I just was not sure
how practical it would be to apply within my time limit to prepare
for the assessment. The professor also brought up the question of
why the New York State curriculum has an entire unit entitled the
Jacksonian Era. No other president has an era named after him.

There is no Roosevelt Era, no Kennedy Era, no Bush Era. Why did Jackson get all of the attention? Once again, I recognized that this was an important concept for my students to understand. However, as far as I was concerned, it was not realistic for me to even consider using in my classroom. My kids probably would not be able to comprehend it.

Despite all of these great ideas, I still struggled to see how these goals could be reached with so many curricular constraints and standardized assessments. I could not always teach what I wanted to teach. I was not teaching an elective. I had no power over the content or the assessment. I could not control which students were placed in my classroom. I would just have to accept that these ideas were best practices and not meant for me to use in the real world. Maybe when the focus on standardized tests disappeared, I would be able to experiment with these educational theories.

Then, one night during this class, I finally had an epiphany. The class was discussing a reading about a young teacher in a local school district. Instead of focusing exclusively on the assessment, she had gone above and beyond what needed to be taught for the test. She had developed units focused on big ideas, created lessons based on student interest, and generally expected a great deal from her students. Her students not only enjoyed the class and felt empowered by the ways in which she chose to teach them, but they also succeeded on the state assessment. At one point in the discussion, someone brought up a question about the emphasis that many districts place on teaching to the test and how much we would really be able to teach like this woman without being criticized. I remember the professor looking at all of us and saying, "Some teachers are scared to move away from teaching to the test. But shouldn't you be scared not to?"

It was as if someone had jolted me awake from a nightmare. I thought about what I had done to my classroom just because of one academically low class of students and because I was afraid of how my special education students would react to being challenged in new ways. Suddenly, I knew that I had made a mistake. I had seen students struggling with the large, overarching questions and I had not thought to take the time to show students how to work with big ideas. I had been impatient and, as a result, had abandoned what would have probably helped these students to connect to and understand the content in a more global way. They were not going to always comprehend or remember all the specific details of history, but they were capable of grasping main themes and thinking actively about the past. I could not go back and change what I had done, but I could do something about my classroom now. The school year had just begun a month before, and I had plenty of time to make a difference.

After I came home from class, I rushed to my computer and began typing up a proposal for change. I designed a contract for my students to sign that explained how class would be structured from now on. I wrote how there would be fewer document-based question (DBQ) practice tests, pen-and-paper tests, and lectures. We would be doing more hands-on activities, more units based on big ideas, and more authentic assessments. The one condition was that they needed to put forth their best effort and be willing to work on some challenging tasks in class. Everyone in every class would sign a class contract and I would keep each copy for future reference. I had decided that if I did not implement these changes right way, I would never do so. I was a little nervous about restructuring my units and lessons, but I knew it was for the better. I had two inclusion classes this year and I was not going to underestimate the abilities of the special education students this time. I would adjust my ideas as needed, but I would not resign myself to simply covering the content.

In the morning, I went to my classroom and immediately rearranged the desks. They had been in rows and now I moved them into a "U" shape for discussions. I then found bags of short Popsicle sticks that I had shoved into a cabinet in the back of the room. I had always wanted to use Popsicle sticks to draw names for class discussion and group placements. I would have each student fill one out and use it today for the lesson on elections. Amazingly, most students welcomed the proposal for change and thought that the Popsicle sticks were an interesting idea. One student even mentioned how open and inviting the room looked now with the desks in a new formation.

For the remainder of the class, we looked at documents and had a long discussion on some key questions related to elections. The goal of the lesson was to have students determine whether or not the U.S. government should reform election practices and policies. Since I was not looking for a specific answer for any of the questions, students felt comfortable considering all of the options for each question. These were not simple questions at all. For example, in one inclusion class, we spent almost the whole class talking about whether third parties should exist since they do not often win seats in Congress or the presidential vote. To say the least, I was at once shocked and satisfied. It felt like my first year all over again.

Soon, I started using big ideas to construct each unit. Instead of simply following history in chronological order, I began to group events and people based on themes. Working with the other grade 8 social studies teacher, I helped to develop a new experimental curriculum. I had told him about what I had learned in my graduate class and how it could actually improve our assessment scores by making students think globally about what they were learning. As he also had a broad range of students at different academic levels, he was open to the idea and we promised to exchange thoughts on the success of our big idea units.

Using the New York State social studies curriculum as well as my students' interests and needs, I restructured my units as shown in table 6.1. At first, the students were a bit perplexed when we moved from one unit to the next because they were used to covering different time periods in order. I remember one student saying, "Wait, Miss Foels! Didn't we just talk about the 1960s and now we're back in the 1800s? I'm lost." However, I remained patient and slowly helped them to see that we were focusing on themes instead of eras. I kept the big idea question on the board throughout each unit so that students could refer to it as needed, and I created journal entries that required students to start reflecting on the theme of the unit as we continued learning more about it. I refused to allow students to fail at these tasks and they succeeded.

Table 6.1. Big Idea Units

Big Ideas Unit/Question	Correlation with New York State Curriculum
To what extent have the lives and rights of African Americans changed after the Civil War? Have they gotten better, worse, or have they stayed the same?	Unit 6: Division and Reunion; Unit 7: An Industrial Society; Unit 9: The United States between the Wars; Unit 11: The Changing Nature of the American People from World War II to the Present
Survivor: America! Western Migrants vs. Immigrants. What challenges did each of these groups face and who had better strategies with which to meet these challenges?	Unit 7: An Industrial Society
How has our economy changed over the past 100 years? Are we better off than we once were in terms of labor rights, consumer safety, and economic security?	Unit 7: An Industrial Society; Unit 9: The United States between the Wars
War: What Is It Good For? What makes a war justifiable? What makes us perceive that a war is either "good" or "bad" for America and other countries?	Unit 8: The United States as an Independent Nation in an Increasingly Interdependent World; Unit 10: The United States Assumes Worldwide Responsibilities; Unit 11: The Changing Nature of the American People from World War II to the Present
Can we trust the government and the Constitution to protect our individual rights?	Unit 11: The Changing Nature of the American People from World War II to the Present

CONCLUSION

Though it was initially difficult to change how I thought about and constructed units in this normally chronological course, I was surprised at how easy creating big ideas became over time. After completing my first unit, and seeing that students were able to successfully demonstrate their understanding of the big idea, I was excited to develop more units. Most importantly, I realized that no one was left out of the learning experience. Both regular education and special education students were actively participating in our more student-centered class. The units seemed to help students at a variety of academic levels understand the general themes that appear in U.S. history and made it easier for them to connect specific details together to better memorize facts for the assessment.

Of course, this would not have been possible without the constant support of my colleagues, including the other grade 8 social studies teacher and my two consultant teachers. Thanks to their flexibility and understanding that this change in the curriculum was an experiment for the benefit of the students, I was able to transform theories into realities. In the end, they agreed that the themes worked well, especially for special education students who might have had difficulty keeping track of information based solely on chronology. While our assessment scores did not change significantly from previous years, we recognized the importance of making history more meaningful and relevant to students. On an exit survey at the end of the year, most students reported that they felt they had learned to think about history more in my class, and they thought the themes were useful for organizing and discussing social studies concepts. Those comments were more important to me than any assessment scores could ever have been.

At the beginning of the year, I always decorate my bulletin board with inspirational quotes to motivate students. From now on, there is one that I will be very proud to post up each year because I can relate to it after restructuring my classroom. It is a quote from Mohandas Gandhi that reads, "You must be the change you wish to see in the world." Instead of attempting to improve scores by teaching to the test, we as teachers really need to start considering what ideas and skills are important for students to understand in social studies. In essence, the test is merely one measure of our students' knowledge and does not have as much absolute value as perceived by those in the educational community. It is our job to make history important and interesting for our students. We cannot blame our problems and fears on a test. We must embody students with the power to think and to love learning, to see that they have the ability to shape the future. So be the change you wish to see. Start experimenting with more meaningful big ideas in your classroom. Wouldn't you be scared not to?

REFERENCE

Davidson, J., & Lytle, M. (2000). *After the fact: The art of historical detection.* New York: Knopf.

7

BIG IDEAS AND TECHNOLOGY: A METHODOLOGY TO ENGAGE STUDENTS

Julie Doyle

I was a late bloomer when it came to academics. A lack of readiness, maturity, and a myriad of other factors delayed the academic passion I possess today. The tipping point for me was a political philosophy professor in my undergraduate program who introduced me to the big questions of life such as "What creates change?" and "Are people born good?" This experience pushed me to seriously search for the answers, and before I knew it, I could not get enough of Hegel, Kant, Plato, and Nietzsche. Those questions also opened up my world. Soon I was connecting the works of these dead philosophers with my own experiences and with other disciplines, all of which helped me approach my studies with a newfound confidence. I became a real student that year, and my grades started to reflect my true potential, resulting in a sense of achievement that had incredible ripple effects in all areas of my life.

Upon graduation, however, I had no particular vocation in mind, so I did what most did in my family—I moved around the country and tried out different professions. From a direct-service position in a home for juvenile delinquent boys in Denver, Colorado, to development work for an international microfinance institution in Washington, D.C., I never lost sight of the big questions. While working with delinquent youth, I constantly explored the root causes of delinquency so that I could become better at my work. I wanted to better understand why a young man who was exhibiting success and the potential to graduate from a program would suddenly sabotage all of his accomplishments. While working in international micro-finance, I became interested in how the poorest of the poor learn and value the concept of saving money. What causes some to spend without awareness or regard for consequences, whereas others hold on to and invest their money? I explored these questions because I wanted to become better at my job and I believed examining the root causes was the only way to transcend the day-to-day grind that can result in complacency. When I turned those questions on my own life, I found myself asking, "What is my calling? What profession will make me most happy? In what profession can I best put my talents to work?" I answered each question with a single word: teaching. I realized that I had been teaching in all of my job experiences, from helping explain a computer issue to a co-worker, to helping a young man with his schoolwork. And so the journey of becoming an educator began with asking and answering the big questions. For me, these questions were more than a method to provoke academic engagement in the classroom—they represented an approach to life.

I was first introduced to the concept of teaching with big ideas in a social studies methods class in my graduate teacher preparation program. The professor (Jill Gradwell) presented this methodology as a way to provoke student inquiry and to bring units alive. I was sold. Big idea thinking was not only the methodology with which I approached my life but the methodology that engaged an "I'm happy with a C, just strive not to fall asleep" college student. Some students in the class challenged the concept, arguing, for example, that the New York State curriculum and testing program were too restrictive: There was barely enough time to teach the facts; there was no time to teach students to become historians. At this point, my only teaching experiences had been as a long-term sub in inner-city Buffalo schools, so I understood the criticisms. I knew how hard it was to finish any unit of study, much less a unit that encouraged students to engage with historical ideas. Still, I wholeheartedly believed that teaching with big ideas was a goal worth striving for.

After being hired at Akron Central High School in 2005, I expected to see this methodology light up the faces up apathetic youth, provoke the gifted child to work harder, and cause parents to wonder where I had been hiding. That didn't happen. What happened was much more true to real life. There was no miracle, but I have seen an increase in the number of engaged students, and that has inspired me to use this methodology more and more.

TEACHING IN RURAL NEW YORK

The Akron Central School District is located in Akron, a small, rural village in western New York. The district crosses three counties (Erie, Genesee, and Niagara) and is partially located on the Tonawanda Indian reservation.

The high school has approximately 545 students, and 90 percent are white, 9 percent Native American, and less than 1 percent other minorities. Approximately 26 percent of the student population is eligible for free/reduced lunch, making it a fairly economically diverse school system. As a third-year teacher in this system, I have witnessed some divisions between the Native American and European American students; however, this situation has improved in recent years. Akron invests heavily in maintaining and fostering a good relationship with the Native American community, as evidenced by new teacher orientation trips to the Longhouse and a full-time staff person dedicated to providing support and enrichment opportunities to the Native American population.

Academically, our school performance is quite good, with state Regents exam scores above the state average in all areas except for physics. Our administration is supportive of teachers' instructional needs, as evidenced by professional development opportunities available even amid major budget cuts.

Akron Central is praised for its investment in technology and use of technology to serve instructional needs. All teachers have access to creating their own school-sponsored Web sites, which allow for teachers to create and post podcasts and blogs. Most recently, Akron administrators sent teachers to receive training in a Web-based classroom tool called Moodle. Some teachers have been given Smartboards for use in the classroom and more are being purchased each year. I have high expectations for our technology infrastructure based on my work in other settings that afforded all employees cutting-edge technology. In my classroom, I have a mounted Smartboard with an LCD projector, six student computers, and one teacher computer, and I utilize a Web site for podcasts and blogs. Overall, the technology department seems to be eager to invest in any technology which will better serve the students.

Akron Central High School is an excellent place to work, virtually free of discipline problems that plague many urban and suburban schools. In many ways, Akron is an ideal American school where teachers can really become better at what they do and students are given the opportunity to learn. The only area where I think we can improve is in raising the academic bar. We are not unique, but there seems to be a degree of comfort among students and parents for mediocre grades.

THE RATIONALE FOR MY UNIT

As an example of how I use big ideas, in March 2007 I crafted a unit on nineteenth-century European imperialism around a central question: "Does imperialism help or hurt native people?" I implemented this set of lessons over ten days with grade 10 global history and geography Regents and honors students. The unit covered multiple examples of European imperialism in various regions of Africa and Asia.

The unit on imperialism is part of the New York State global history and geography 10 curriculum. Specifically, this unit falls under unit five: Age of Revolutions (1750–1914), standards 2, 3,

4, and 5. At the end of the grade 10 global history and geography course, students take a comprehensive state Regents examination assessing their knowledge of world history over the course of two years.

I have found in the past that this unit can become quite confusing if not centered around a common theme or question. My big idea—Does imperialism help or hurt native people?—challenged students to examine the effects of imperialism, such as the construction of roads and forced planting of cash crops, in order to determine the effects—both beneficial and detrimental—on native populations.

I chose this particular topic because, with an increasing global world, the tendency for stronger nations to control weaker nations is not only likely but a certainty. The topic of imperialism provokes numerous questions. Given my students' ideas and experiences and the values I hold as a teacher, I believed it was important to develop a big idea that appealed to their strong sense of justice and offered them the opportunity to evaluate policies from multiple perspectives. Rather than merely asking my students to define imperialism and evaluate that policy from the stronger nation's perspective, I encouraged students to evaluate policy by challenging them to always ask, "Whom does this policy benefit and how?" and "Who does not benefit from this policy and why not?" When we provoke this type of analysis with our students, we prepare them to view the world with a smart, critical lens.

I have found that when my students take on the big questions of history, they become engaged, make connections, and acquire confidence as they become more than humble consumers of historical material. As students wrestle with big ideas, they develop the ability to approach the media with a critical eye. Our media are increasingly profit driven and sensationalized, and teachers have a responsibility to educate students about this reality. We must model and provide opportunities for students to critically think about history, so that they apply this approach to academic studies as well as to their life experiences. When I utilized the big idea approach coupled with the use of technology, my students found new ways to become engaged in their studies.

A BIG IDEA UNIT AROUND IMPERIALISM

To address the big idea of whether imperialism helps or hurts native people, I divided the unit into the following five sets of lessons:

1. Introduction to nineteenth-century imperialism. Two forty-minute periods.
2. Imperialism in Africa. Two forty-minute periods.
3. Imperialism in India. Two forty-minute periods.
4. Imperialism in the Middle East. Two forty-minute periods.
5. Assessment. One forty-minute period in-class test and one forty-minute period featuring a document-based question task.

To ensure that I addressed the big question throughout the unit, I designed all in-class and out-of-class activities around this central question. Doing so allowed me to organize numerous historical events under one central theme—imperialism. For the purpose of this chapter, I share some of my insights from the introductory and Africa sections. From my observations of classroom discussion and my analysis of student Web postings and notebook responses, I found that students made strong connections in history across different places, cultures, and time periods; they viewed history through multiple perspectives; and they voiced their beliefs and opinions frequently. On top of that, their local and state test scores demonstrated that they knew and understood the ideas in ways that are more easily measured.

STUDENTS MAKING STRONG CONNECTIONS TO HISTORY

Making history relevant to students is absolutely paramount for me. I think one way to make strong connections is by helping them see the relationships between current and historical issues and events. If teachers highlight these relationships, students are more likely to retain historical ideas and to be able to see historical concepts as events unfold in our world.

My first unit lesson introduced the construct of imperialism and the big idea for the unit. We began by reviewing several definitions of imperialism available on online dictionary sites (merriam-webster .com and dictionary.com). We then selected one definition of imperialism to use throughout the unit: "A stronger nation controlling a weaker nation for political, social, and/or economic reasons." Later, I shared photos that illustrated some of the effects imperialism has had on different areas of the world. The pictures included both positive effects such as construction of roads and negative effects such as the forced planting of cash crops. At that point, I introduced the big idea with the observation that people offer differing viewpoints on whether imperialism helps or hurts native peoples. I explained we would continually revisit this question and that the students would be able to defend their answers throughout the unit. In the last portion of the introduction, I had the students listen to a National Public Radio audio recording of a speech by Hugo Chavez accusing the United States of practicing imperialism. I then asked the students to respond to several questions by posting a commentary to my blog on the school Web site (see figure 7.1).

Although all students were equipped with the same definition of imperialism, their perceptions of imperialism and their assessment of the war in Iraq, for example, varied considerably. For instance, Shannon wrote, "If we went to Iraq for the purpose of overthrowing Saddam Hussein and ridding the country of WMDs . . . but we have remained there to try and form a stable government and our own way of life . . . then yes, I feel the U.S. is practicing imperialism in Iraq." Shannon's response reflects an ability to connect the concept of imperialism, as learned in the introductory nineteenth-century imperialism lesson, with her understanding of what the United States is doing in Iraq today. Her classmate Adam viewed the situation in Iraq differently: "I disagree with everyone in saying the U.S. is an imperialist nation. If the U.S. were imperialist, why would we try and set up a form of self-government for the Iraqis?" Adam's response reflects an ability to differentiate between simply installing a government or a way of life and helping "set up a form of self-government." Lastly, Sarah's response represents an understanding of both the positive and

```
┌─────────────────────────────────────────────────────┐
│                                                       │
│             IMPERIALISM BLOG ASSIGNMENT               │
│                (posted on teacher website)            │
│                                                       │
│   Step 1: Listen to the NPR broadcast at:             │
│   http://www.npr.org/templates/story/story.php?storyId=6423000 │
│                                                       │
│   Step 2: Acquaint yourself with the definition of imperialism. While │
│   listening, please take notes on the following questions: │
│                                                       │
│   •   What groups have recently referred to the U.S. as │
│       imperialist?                                    │
│                                                       │
│   •   Historically, how does the U.S. feel about being referred to │
│       as imperialist?                                 │
│                                                       │
│   •   Newt Gingrich says that the U.S. IS an imperial power—but │
│       what kind? In what way?                         │
│                                                       │
│   •   What does Harvard historian Neil Ferguson indicate as the │
│       reason why the U.S. has trouble with the word imperial? │
│                                                       │
│   Step 3: Click on the hyperlink post a comment. Please respond │
│   to the following questions in your response:        │
│                                                       │
│   •   Do you think the U.S. practices imperialism? (according to │
│       the definition) Why?                            │
│                                                       │
│   •   Depending on your response to Q#1, do you think the U.S. │
│       should or should not practice imperialism? Why or why not? │
│                                                       │
└─────────────────────────────────────────────────────┘
```

Figure 7.1.   Imperialism Blog Assignment

negative ramifications of a policy of imperialism: "The U.S. practices imperialism, but I do believe it will benefit our world in the long run . . . helping to establish equal rights, lower the risk of nuclear weapons . . . however if we continue to force our culture, we will lose the possibility of using ideas of other nations to improve ours."

The blogging technology was a useful means for students to convey their understanding of modern-day imperialism. Because the big idea question was open ended and designed to transcend a single era, students were able to offer a variety of opinions about imperialism and draw conclusions about the current U.S. involvement in Iraq. I did not instruct the students to focus on the war in Iraq, but they gravitated to this example as it is the current event with which they are most familiar. In the future, I may present several current events for the students to utilize in generating their responses to the blog in order to offer diversity in assessing the concept of imperialism across different places, cultures, and time periods.

STUDENTS VIEWING HISTORY THROUGH MULTIPLE PERSPECTIVES

Evaluating history through multiple perspectives requires students to look at policies and how they impact various groups of people. The methodology requires providing students with ample primary source accounts that illustrate the varying effects of policies like imperialism. Looking at policies through multiple perspectives not only encourages empathy for others but generates a more nuanced and enriched picture of history.

During the section on imperialism in Africa, I reintroduced the big idea as an introductory question and distributed packets of photographs. Students viewed pictures of the Belgian Congo such as the enslaved Congolese, elephants, piles of ivory tusks, and Belgian officials supervising the extraction of ivory. For each picture, I posed two questions: (1) What do you think the Belgians' motives were in this region and (2) How did this interest impact the Congolese people? The second day of this lesson, we examined the Berlin Conference—who attended, what they decided, and what the impact was. Students then examined what imperialism looked like in other African regions, such as Nigeria, where tribal lines divided due to the Berlin Conference and roads were built. At the end of class, students responded to the following question in the quiz section

---

**IMPACT OF IMPERIALISM
BLOG ASSIGNMENT**

WHAT? Using the Internet, find information regarding the impact that European imperialism has on Africa today (the people, economy, government, tribes, etc.). Find information that illustrates the impact (positive OR negative) on any people, region, tribe, etc., in Africa.

WHERE? DO NOT use Wikipedia, excerpts from online term papers, etc. DO USE .edu, .gov sites, etc.

HOW? In your posting, include the following:

- The region and people you are describing and the European imperial power (e.g., Nigeria and Britain)

- The impact today (meaning the last fifty yrs)

- Whether you believe the impact has been positive or negative and why.

- One link to a website where you found your information

NOTE: Be creative! Remember, we want to SEE the impact and understand it. Therefore, be concise and make it interesting.

Figure 7.2. Impact of Imperialism Blog Assignment

of their notebook: "Does imperialism help or hurt native people? Please cite one region in Africa and provide two examples to defend your response." At the conclusion of the lesson on imperialism in Africa, students were asked to respond to the blog assignment shown in figure 7.2.

The majority of students cited excerpts from sources that illustrated imperialism through native eyes. For instance, Rachel selected a journal entry describing the impact of French colonization in Algeria: "Massacres of women, children . . . torching villages and harvests." Not surprisingly, she concluded that "French imperialism had a negative effect on Algeria." Mallory cited the Congolese undeveloped industries and dependence on imports as evidence that imperialism had a "negative effect." Nicole offered a particularly interesting analysis of imperialism in Ethiopia: "Most people believe that imperialism is horrible, and that it destroys people's sense of self and livelihood . . . but the people of Ethiopia banded together . . . aiding the unification of a nation." Nicole's analysis reflects an understanding of how adversity can result in empowerment. Chelsea, on the other hand, cited how British imperialism in Nigeria "contributed to Nigerian development." She concluded that "imperialism can be positive." Mary chose to evaluate the environmental perspective, citing how "fish have either moved to a healthier zone or have died . . . due to oil spills . . . " from British imperialism in Nigeria.

In addition to being able to choose their own perspectives with which to evaluate imperialism, students benefited from viewing the other perspectives offered by their classmates. Judging from the majority "native perspectives" selections in the blogs, I believe the assignment "research the impact of European imperialism" set them up to find more native perspectives. After thinking more about this result and after looking at all the blogs as a whole, I realized that the students expressed their impressions of imperialism through the multiple perspectives of the native groups rather than through a European lens. Big idea questions allow for students to consider history from multiple vantage points. If those questions are not presented in a sufficiently open-ended manner, however, they can drive students to consider select viewpoints. In the future, I will assist more with Internet research techniques, such as "positive and negative impacts of imperialism," to help them generate more diversity in their Internet findings.

Through a blog assignment driven by big idea questions, my students offered rich, unique, and insightful assessments on the impact of imperialism. From looking at imperialism and its impact on people to the impact it has had on the environment, students proved not only that they are capable of assessing history but that they are also able to approach historical events from multiple perspectives.

INCREASE IN STUDENT VOICE DUE TO
BLOG TECHNOLOGY

Student voice is critical in education. We need to understand what our students know, what they want to know, and what they have learned. Often the use of Socratic methods in the traditional classroom setting limits the voice of some students. While the skill of presenting oral arguments should always be encouraged and expected in the classroom, blog assignments can offer less verbal students a chance to have their voices heard, provide time for students to process historical information and convey it in richer forms, and encourage student ownership of their learning.

Through the course of the many blog assignments, I was able to hear the voices of many of my students. For instance, I was surprised at Laura's posting in her blog: "There is no way to say for sure the Iraqi people are benefiting from our actions. Personally, I believe they are not, because many of them have been killed. The U.S. should not practice imperialism . . . nor should any other nation." Prior to reading her response, I had no idea that Laura held such passionate beliefs about world politics. I was similarly amazed at Matt's posting: "Europeans brought these ideas into Africa that white people are better than black people . . . and that is what I believe caused the most harm to Africa." Like Laura, Matt rarely said much in class, but it was clear from his blog response that Matt held some very strong beliefs and that he felt comfortable sharing them so bluntly.

Blogs seemed to encourage students to articulate their positions in more thoughtful ways when compared to the manner in which they relayed information during class discussions. For example, Chelsea pointed out that "British imperialism in Nigeria illustrates how imperialism can contribute to an area's development but, at the same time, hinder an area's resources and individuality." Chelsea's assessment illustrates an ability to see the nuances of history, principally that historical events can have both positive and negative effects. Mallory, normally a painfully shy student who typically offered only one- or two-word responses during class discussions, said that "the people of the Congo have been prevented from developing their own industries . . . so they had to depend on imports which were controlled by industrialized nations . . . causing them to go into debt . . . and take out more loans . . . this shows the negative impact of imperialism." Mallory's assessment shows a sophisticated understanding of what causes some newly independent nations to remain impoverished. Blogs provided an outlet for students like Chelsea and Mallory to share deep, meaningful ideas about issues related to European imperialism, which they may not have shared during a traditional in-class discussion.

The understanding with which I established the blog assignments was that students would send their comments to me via Intranet, after which I approved them for public display on the Smartboard the following day. I think this understanding that their peers would be viewing their posting encouraged students to invest in the assignment. For classroom discussion, I selected various postings to discuss in class, making sure to include the more quiet students who had offered interesting insights. The student eagerness to discuss their blog comments was due, I believe, to the fact that they were able to invest effort into their postings and were generally proud of their work. With access to Smartboard markers, I was able to circle interesting points as we read through their postings and put question marks next to parts that needed elaboration. Overall, blogging offered the less verbal students the opportunity to voice their opinions, and the Smartboard served as a springboard to discuss their opinions in a traditional classroom setting.

I must add a side benefit of the blog comments and discussions: they were tremendously enjoyable for me as the teacher, as this level of conversation is so rare in a sophomore class. That said, the blogging was not an end in itself. The open-ended big idea questions made the difference. When questions are too narrowly crafted, students' responses follow, as was the case where I directed the students to consider only native perspectives. I found that great, engaging discussions are possible with fifteen-year-old and sixteen-year-old students if, and only if, the students engage with the questions I pose.

Overall, I believe teaching with big ideas increases the likelihood of engaging students and increasing their historical knowledge and understanding. Student engagement can look different from student to student. For the quiet student, engagement can simply be a raised hand in response to a question posed; for the more verbal student, engagement can be the public connection of a historical concept to a recent current event. However it manifests, engaging my students seems to pay off: they performed better on the state global history and geography exam than their peers across the state. Of the 170 regular and special education students who were tested, 91 percent scored 55 or higher, 80 percent scored 65 or higher, and 35 percent achieved mastery (85 or higher). By comparison, 77 percent of all tested students scored 55 or higher, 63 percent scored 65 or higher, and 24 percent achieved mastery across the state.

CONCLUSION

Overall, I believe teaching with big ideas increases the likelihood of engaging students. The challenge for me as a teacher was to recognize the opportunity to engage a student, reflect on what triggered that opportunity, and continue to afford my students engaging opportunities.

While teaching the unit on imperialism, I reached the following conclusions on teaching with big ideas: (1) students made strong connections from the past to the present, (2) they were better able to view multiple perspectives (natives vs. Europeans, as well as their peers' perspectives), and (3) they took advantage of the opportunity to add their voices to the classroom discussions (more likely to make evidenced-based arguments, speak up, express complex thoughts) due to access to blog technology.

As I continue to improve as a teacher and to develop more units framed around big ideas, there are several questions I carry with me. Can teaching with big ideas be attained in all units of study? Can poorly planned big idea units cause teachers to oversimplify historical information or, much worse, manipulate history to fit the big idea? If teaching with big ideas requires rigorous planning, do our standard preparatory periods that are consumed with student concerns and correcting papers allow for such thoughtful planning?

I think continuing to examine these questions is very important so that we can realistically consider this big idea methodology in the field of education. At the same time, the benefits of teaching with big ideas are enormous. As a young, disengaged college student, I was awakened when my professor used big ideas. When I responded to big questions, I was both validated and challenged, and with that experience my journey as a student began. I think all of our students deserve this opportunity, no matter how difficult it may be.

8

RECONSTRUCTING RECONSTRUCTION AND HISTORY

Mary Beth Bruce

When some teachers hear the words "Advanced Placement," they conjure up images of a course that looks a lot like nirvana, a course where students are eager to learn, achieve high grades, and demonstrate a level of intellect, maturity, and motivation. Conversely, others picture a course with a curriculum that is far too extensive, detail oriented, and cumbersome and students who are obsessed with grades, have overly eager parents, and demand constant attention and direction. When many teachers think about teaching Advanced Placement, they often perceive the amount of content to be taught as burdensome. They feel pressured to cover the material without exploring in depth the major ideas or concepts prevalent throughout a unit of study. It is most often these same educators who rely on lecture and PowerPoint presentations to make it through the course. It is my contention that in order for a student to truly know and understand what happened in the past, teachers must help students formulate a framework for that knowledge and understanding. It is my assertion that big ideas are the ideal framework for quality teaching and learning and that this pedagogical strategy can be utilized effectively in any classroom setting, regardless of whether the pressure for content coverage exists.

Using big ideas in a social studies classroom is a concept I was introduced to early in my studies at the University at Buffalo's Graduate School of Education. The first graduate-level education class I enrolled in was Methods of Teaching Social Studies. I was exposed to a great deal of theory regarding the best practices of teaching social studies. I read a lot of research regarding curriculum design and assessment. I enjoyed having philosophical conversations about whether teachers ever really know what a student knows. These conversations intrigued me and I was very excited about my new career choice.

Then came the reality of actually implementing what I had read. The first homework assignment for this class was to create a lesson plan on Gandhi. Needless to say, I was a bit stumped, never before having seen an actual lesson plan. I received my BA in history and physical geography, so being asked the best way to engage students for a one-day lesson on Gandhi was a challenge. It was at that point I knew there was plenty about teaching and learning that I needed to learn, and I recall feeling that I was in for an eye-opening experience.

It was during the next class that I was introduced to the concept of the big idea. Some of the students in the class caught on right away, for they immediately began creating thought-provoking questions focused around people such as Queen Elizabeth and Frederick Douglass and around events such as the civil rights movement. To be honest, I didn't get it at all at first and was actually quite hesitant to utilize and implement this pedagogical strategy. I originally perceived the big idea as a catchphrase or fancy title for a unit; the concept just didn't quite click. I am a bit embarrassed to recall that the first big idea I created, for a unit on the Great Depression, focused on something about a "downward spiral spiraling up, up, and away." Bizarre, I know, but I remained positive and open-minded and was determined to persevere through my misunderstanding.

As time went on, however, I grew increasingly frustrated that the big ideas I created were not getting any better; they were not at all thought provoking or even catchy. It took some time for me to learn to think "big" about teaching social studies. But I vividly remember the day that I finally got it, the day that the concept clicked. My re-action was "How did I *not* get this?" The big idea I devised was for a U.S. history unit centered on Cold War foreign policy. My overarch-ing question: "Was containment of the Reds worth the bloodshed?" I thought this question worked because it provided a focus for my unit and lesson plans; it was a question I could pose to my students that was intriguing and thought provoking, and it allowed my stu-dents to focus their understanding and formulate an interpretation about the topic. After I taught the unit, I was extremely satisfied with the work the students produced. I was happy with their ability to make connections and take a stand on issues surrounding this era of history. Therefore, I quickly learned that it does make sense to use big ideas as overarching frameworks for unit design. And yes, I did realize that they are *much* more than fun catchphrases and fancy titles for units. Please understand, however, that it actually took me a full year of teaching in a classroom before I felt that I was actually any good at creating big idea questions, not to mention implementing them in a thoughtful manner.

Today, I cannot imagine teaching without using big ideas. When I go about planning units, I always begin with the end in mind and have thus far created big ideas as frameworks for unit design for every unit I have taught, ranging from U.S. history and government, AP U.S. history, participation in government, and an elective titled Women in American Society. Simply put, it's a method that works.

THE SCHOOL CONTEXT

I teach at Sweet Home High School, a community school located in the Sweet Home Central School District. The district, which consists of four elementary schools, one middle school, and one high school, is a K–12 public school district located in the towns of Amherst and Tonawanda, northern suburbs of Buffalo, New York. The high school population is approximately 1,277 students.

Sweet Home is a full inclusion school. This means that all students with special needs are mainstreamed into general education classrooms throughout the entire day or for parts of the school day. We also have small, self-contained classes and special programs for ESL students and adults in the neighborhood.

The Sweet Home school district has a diverse racial, ethnic, and socioeconomic composition. Twenty-six percent of our students are eligible for free and reduced lunch. The school's population is about 15 percent African American, 3 percent Hispanic, 3 percent Asian, and almost 79 percent white.

The Sweet Home school district values its diversity and is dedicated to reaching all learners in our classrooms. Many professional development courses are available through our local Teacher Center to educate staff on current research and best practices, and teachers are encouraged to work on teams to collaborate and share their best practices. Sweet Home is *not* one of the most affluent districts in western New York, but in my view, it is successful because of its diversity. At Sweet Home, we consider ourselves one of the biggest overachieving school districts when compared to local area schools.

The pressure placed on teachers to get students to perform well on state tests is more implicit than explicit. At my school, approximately 97 percent of our students pass the grade 11 state exam in U.S. history and government, and approximately 92 percent of the students pass the grade 10 exam in global history and geography. Approximately 64 percent of those students who take the U.S. history and government exam and 37 percent of those who take the global history and geography exam achieve what the state deems mastery of the subject matter. In spite of our departmental success, many of my colleagues feel the pressure to improve our passing and mastery rates. Therefore, the reality of teacher accountability and the anxiety that coincides with it definitely exists.

Many of my colleagues employ ambitious teaching strategies, but most do so in elective courses or courses that have no state test at the end of the year. Yes, we all create and utilize performance tasks and formative assessments in an effort to keep students challenged and engaged, but the pressure to cover content is real and does cause some teachers to be more didactic. Why would anyone want to follow such a demoralizing instructional path? Possibly because at the end of each school year, the district administrators provide each teacher with a detailed spreadsheet that lists the passing rates by percentage for all students (male, female, IEP, and 504 Plans) enrolled in our classes. In addition, on the last day of the scheduled school year, all teachers participate in what is called "data day." On this day, our administrators hand out to each teacher detailed analyses of all Regents multiple-choice questions broken down by the percentage of students who got each question right and wrong. It should be obvious that this type of micromanaged accountability can cause some teachers to focus on direct instruction as a means of achieving desired test results rather than on the deeper understandings of history.

Although researchers have shown that teaching in didactic ways, teaching test-taking skills, and teaching only testlike content (i.e., content that continually appears on the Regents exam) are inconsistent with deeper understandings of historical thought, some teachers, especially nontenured teachers, do it anyway. I think they feel, as I have, that there is not enough time to be ambitious and innovative. Consequently, the pressure to cover content becomes a quasi-security blanket. And what appears to be ironic is that, although district administrators seem to support more ambitious teaching through the use of big ideas and performance tasks, on the last day of school, the only things celebrated are Regents exam results. It is no wonder, then, that faculty perceive mixed messages coming from the administration.

Currently, I teach Advanced Placement U.S. history and a women's studies elective at the high school. Both are courses that students elect to take to earn social studies credits for graduation. I have taught Regents U.S. history and government, and one of the biggest differences in teaching AP is the level of detail in the curriculum. The students are responsible for knowing, understanding, and mastering a depth and breadth of content and skills that far exceed a Regents-level course. The pressure to cover material is even stronger in an AP course than in a Regents-level class, and the difference in the testing schedules exacerbates the problem: The Regents tests are administered during the second or third week of June, while the AP exam is usually administered during the first week in May. So AP teachers are expected to teach almost twice as much content and skills as their Regents peers but in five weeks less time. When I thought about how I was going to tackle this seemingly daunting task, I decided to go with what worked in the past, and that was creating units centered on large concepts or big ideas.

As I took on the challenge of teaching AP, it also made sense to focus on historiography, or the art of historical inquiry, as I had in my Regents courses. Although my background as a history major as an undergraduate largely influenced this choice, I believed it was important to teach kids how history is constructed and interpreted. I wanted kids to learn more than the chronology and facts of the past and the epic travels of our Founding Fathers and Mothers. I wanted them to "do" history, to analyze documents from the past, to determine their authenticity, and to formulate their own views about events.

When I entered college, a persistent feeling that I was never taught how history is actually written and constructed upset me. My first history class focused on the Vietnam War. The instructor had the entire class engaged in inquiry-oriented endeavors. Never before did I, as a student in a history class, have so much ownership over what I learned; my elementary and secondary educational career did not prepare me for or expose me to the art of historical inquiry. My teachers did not prepare me for the reality that history is a living science, an investigative process. I was always "good" at social studies; I always enjoyed the subject and liked the competition involved with getting the answers right. It was my college professors, however, who taught me that history is subject to multiple interpretation and that there is not always a right answer. This idea intrigued me and brought my interest for the subject to a new level. I wanted to share this knowledge and enthusiasm with my students, so I have always made historical inquiry a part of my classes, and using big ideas helps me do that.

A HISTORIOGRAPHY PROJECT

In a continuing effort to help students think like historians, I created a series of activities designed to motivate them to think critically about the Reconstruction era. My students had just finished studying a unit centered around two big ideas: "Reconstruction: America's Unfinished Revolution?" and "Reconstruction: A Race to Reunite or a Never-ending Fight?" In that unit, I asked my students to analyze primary, secondary, and tertiary materials and to gather evidence, classify it, and categorize it. I asked them to imagine what it was like to be someone else, to live somewhere else—to put themselves in someone else's shoes. Throughout these tasks, I warned the class to be cautious about making judgments based on present-day ideas and beliefs.

As a result of this unit, and upon further reflection, I realized I was overly involved in the knowledge acquisition and learning process. If I really wanted to know what kids know and understand, I was going to have to take a step back and be less controlling over the information that is analyzed and filtered by the students. I realized after reading many of the students' reflections that their responses to the big ideas were simply regurgitations of what historians said about the topics. Few kids presented me with original thoughts about the era, and some, in spite of my advice, continued to view the historical events from a present-day lens. This realization provided the inspiration I needed to take the unit to the next level. What follows is a description of the unit I call a Historiography Workshop. The focus was on students creating their own big ideas and seeking the facts to support their arguments about what really happened during the era of Reconstruction. This academic endeavor proved to me that my students could be successful at the art of historical inquiry.

I thought the tasks created surrounding the prior unit had gone pretty well, and I was satisfied with the knowledge attained. But I wanted to do something to push my students a little further. More specifically, I wanted to help them figure out what questions they still had about the era, how they could find the answers to them, what was the best evidence to use to find those answers, and how one evaluates evidence—essentially, to do exactly what historians do as they develop their research projects. These historiographic questions, interwoven through a series of scaffolding activities, helped students create frameworks for assessing their own understandings about the past. More specifically, I challenged the students to craft their own big ideas and to create their own historical narratives with reference to the Reconstruction era. The students read additional primary, secondary, and tertiary source materials on the era. They then analyzed the sources and engaged in a "Reading for Meaning" activity and a "Compare/Contrast" task to help them craft a historical narrative of their own.

On the surface, some of these activities may appear quite teacher directed, but I believe it is our duty to create activities to focus students' learning and understanding in an effort to get them thinking about writing history. Therefore, these structured assignments were an attempt to provide the students with a series of scaffolded activities that were not an end in themselves but instead were meant to offer a place from which kids could launch their own inquiries. It was an attempt to help the students make sense of contrasting viewpoints and to help them see how experts in the field may organize and solve problems. It was through these activities that students demonstrated an understanding of how historians make sense of the past. The point of the exercise was to get the kids thinking in *anticipation* of writing—getting them to take ownership of their learning in an effort to actually "do" history. It was through these activities that some interesting revelations took place.

Day 1: Reading for Meaning

On the first day of the unit, the students analyzed primary source materials and engaged in a "Reading for Meaning" activity. In this activity, I posed statements to the students, they read primary source documents, and they had to agree or disagree with the statements using evidence from the sources. In essence, they had to justify their positions by giving evidence from the text to support their points of view. Some of the statements were:

- The civil rights acts of the Reconstruction era were ineffective.
- Rebuilding the South after the war went relatively smoothly.
- Upon Emancipation, race relations in America improved drastically.
- The system of sharecropping was an effective way to manage the labor system of the South.

The excerpts included pieces from Leon Litwack's *Been in the Storm So Long: The Aftermath of Slavery*, John Q. Anderson's *Brokenburn: The Journal of Kate Stone, 1861–1868*, and Thomas Dixon Jr.'s *The Clansman: An Historical Romance of the Ku Klux Klan*. (For a list of the other sources, see appendix A.)

As the students read the primary sources and responded to the statements, it was great to see that they were able to read, interpret, analyze, categorize, and defend their point of view. For example, when given the statement "The civil rights acts of the Reconstruction era were ineffective," many students defended their views by going back and referencing the documents they were asked to analyze and then went further by reflecting on and incorporating information they had learned during the previous unit. In doing so, they formulated interpretations based on the connections they made between what they knew about race relations, equality, and due process today.

I want to note that, before I had the students read the sources, I reviewed with them what to consider when evaluating and analyzing historical evidence/documents, especially the context in which such sources were written. I had the students consider the following questions: Is what you are reading an excerpt from a larger written piece? What is the author's agenda? Is the source reliable? Is the document significant/relevant? How do you know? I reminded them that understanding who is asking questions and how and by whom they are being answered makes a difference. The analogy I presented was as follows: "Imagine you went to a party with your friends on a Friday evening. When you got home, your parents asked you what you did, if you had fun, and the like. The next day, your best friend, who was not at the party, calls and asks you the same questions. Do you answer your friend the same way you answered your parents?" I use this scenario to stress that facts in isolation are meaningless and that one person's interpretation of an event tells only a fraction of the story.

Keep in mind that I made the students choose whether they agreed or disagreed with the statements listed above. They could acknowledge another point of view, but ultimately they had to choose one side—to agree or disagree with the statements posed. Doing so pushed the students' awareness of their personal beliefs and convictions. It forced them to think more deeply about the content. Some students definitely had a hard time doing this; many still struggled to find the "right" answer. I reassured those few kids that their views *were* the right answers, as long as they justified them with the appropriate evidence. I suspected that they were skeptical about owning a historical view. Put simply, many students lack the intellectual freedom in their social studies classes. They seem to think that, in order to be a historian, one must be a "master memorizer" of facts, dates, names, and locations. This reaction is not surprising, given that many students face a steady diet of multiple-choice assessments.

It was at this point that I reminded the students that history is an art *and* a science, one that involves problem solving about America's past in an effort to understand the present. I reminded them that studying history and creating history can, at times, be uncomfortable and even unkind. Issues such as racism, discrimination, equality, and conformity are all around them; these are things students can relate to, concepts they can relate to because they see them every day.

Day 2: Prior Knowledge Acquisition

On the second day of the unit, the students answered a series of general questions about Reconstruction based solely on their prior knowledge of the era. I divided them into groups and distributed a handout that featured an exhaustive list of questions, about forty all together. The first ten were as follows (for the rest of the questions, see appendix B):

- What questions faced the nation once the war ended?
- In what ways did freedmen define their freedom?
- Assess the goals of the Freedmen's Bureau. Were they realistic for the times?
- What might have happened had the northern and southern Democrats united politically after the Civil War?
- Would you have voted to impeach Johnson? Explain.
- Was the Fifteenth Amendment effective?
- Were the Redeemers in any way justified in their actions?
- Did northern whites have any business getting involved in the politics of the New South?
- In what ways was the Old South resurrected postwar?
- Does nineteenth-century civil rights legislation affect us today?

I did not expect students to answer all of these questions; I asked each group to choose at least ten. Ultimately, the students responded to 90 percent of the questions and did so correctly, meaning that they used evidence to support their points of view. (Those questions left unaddressed during class were assigned for homework.) Then, as a class, we discussed their responses.

This activity proved to be a useful assessment of the previous unit and a useful insight into how students were making sense of the ideas prevalent throughout this unit of study. For example, I was surprised to see how many students defended Andrew Johnson's Reconstruction policies and that several empathized with his dilemma of reuniting the nation after the war. One student highlighted Johnson's use of the pardon:

> I know some in Congress probably regarded Johnson's plan as an abuse of his power; however, he did what he had to do to keep the nation united. His decision to grant a ton of pardons to many ex-Confederates for committing treason is totally understandable, given

the nation was still politically disunited, and we have to keep in mind that he was a southerner himself. I give him credit for being a strong president. I don't know what I would have done.

Other students expressed empathy for a range of people, such as African Americans, carpetbaggers, and radical reformers. One student emphasized the weak role government played in protecting people:

> I feel really bad for those people who were just trying to exercise the rights that the government had granted them. I mean after the Fifteenth Amendment was passed, that's really when the chaos began. The fact that the KKK terrorized all of these groups of people must have been horrifying. It's kind of like the hate crimes that are committed today. I mean, think about it, any coward can hide behind a white sheet and commit acts of violence . . . and think about the fact that the southern state governments turned a blind eye to the violence—it's just criminal.

It was clear that students could see beyond what are often stereotypical views, such as the idea that all Confederates were "bad." Asked whether the Confederate soldiers were heroes, one student remarked that he thought they absolutely could be considered heroes because they fought for and defended a way of life that they believed in:

> If you define a hero as a person who fights for what they believe in, then even though the system of slavery was immoral and degrading, one could argue that it was economically beneficial to the southern economy, and so by freeing up their labor force, the South would surely fall to economic ruin that would last for decades . . . they were just fighting to preserve their way of life.

A few students became frustrated with the ambiguity of some of the questions, such as "Does nineteenth-century civil rights legislation affect us today?" One student's level of frustration reached an apex when he stated, "But we didn't learn anything about race relations and civil rights today!" This is where I had to stop again and entertain a conversation about the inherent big ideas within the exercise. I asked the students to remember what we had talked about earlier regarding racism, friendship, equality, and discrimination. I asked them to consider thinking of history in terms of relationships. And I posed the question "How does the civil rights debate of the Reconstruction era connect to the twentieth-century civil rights movement?" This is where connections were made to racism, civil rights, and equality today. Once again, these are themes that students can relate to. They know what it is like to be treated differently because of what you look like; they know what it is like to be favored because of who you are or what you do. They can relate to concepts such as punishment, consequences, and unfairness. So it was crucial to reinforce these connections here, the idea that even though we have not studied the facts, we all can relate to the emotion.

I interpreted the student's comment to mean that we all learn at different paces, and it is the teacher's role to push all students to think critically in an effort to get them to a deeper level. Clearly, not all students are comfortable with thinking outside the box. Many students, especially honors or AP kids, are used to being told the right answer—they memorize it, get it right on the test, and then forget it. That is how the game of school is played. Sometimes when I challenge students to make connections to current issues, they feel a bit uneasy if they have not read about it in their textbook yet. I wonder if they fear their answer is not going to be right if it's not already written down or validated by someone else.

Day 3: An Interview with the Experts: Comparing and Contrasting Viewpoints

On the third day of the unit, the students analyzed secondary and tertiary materials and completed an "Interview with a Historian" worksheet. They read excerpts from Q&A sessions where historians commented on research they had conducted (these excerpts are available at www.pbs.org) that actually answered the questions I posed to the students during the prior day's activity. The students then had to compare and contrast their own answers with those of the scholars in the field. This activity proved to be a very powerful learning tool, for it validated the convictions and beliefs students had about their findings.

As an example, in the section on deconstructing myths about the era, historian Eric Foner responded to the statement that the Klan was a small group of renegades from southern society:

> Most of the leaders of the Klan were very respectable members of their communities, business leaders, farmers, and ministers. You know, there was sort of a myth, that "Oh, this is just a bunch of young toughs, you know, and the real established southerners wouldn't do this." But actually, in the [Klan] trials it became very clear that they were very respectable people, so to speak. And all that comes out in these hearings and trials. It really puts a face on Klan activity, and you see the victimization and the terrible injustices that have been suffered.

Another example is historian Ted Tunnell's response about how the Reconstruction/civil rights debate connects to the twentieth-century civil rights movement:

> The second Reconstruction is what historians call the civil rights movement of the 1950s and 1960s, the time in which finally black people are truly emancipated. They're only half emancipated after the Civil War. Final emancipation, final meaning to the promise of the first Reconstruction, doesn't come until the 1950s and the 1960s, in the second Reconstruction. But without the first one, you don't have the second. . . .
>
> In some sense, the first Reconstruction is ahead of its time. The public accommodations clauses, the civil rights laws, this notion of a biracial citizenship, that black people are going to be full partners in the story of American life. The promise is there in the first Reconstruction, but it is aborted. And it doesn't fully come to fruition until the second Reconstruction.

Notice that these were answers to the same questions that the students just answered the day before. The students had to support or refute the historians' statements based on the research and reflections completed in class. The students had to challenge the assumptions they had about the era after comparing their responses with those of the historians. For example, when presented with the statement "The Klan was a small group of renegades from southern society," some students were shocked to find out that they were respectable leaders in southern communities, not just "ignorant white trash" as one student had labeled them. Other students were happy to see that their views coincided with a historian's.

The students then completed a written "Compare/Contrast" task. They compared and contrasted their answers to those points of view offered by the historians interviewed. The students had to use information from the "Reading for Meaning" worksheet, the "Interview with a Historian" worksheet, and their knowledge of the era. In other words, the students had to first find similarities and/or consistencies between their research and the historians in the field (and as compared with their textbook and other sources analyzed the week prior). They then found differences and/or inconsistencies. Exploring these contradictions helped challenge their thinking and their preconceived notions about events. When responding to the question "What made rebuilding so hard?" one student at first focused mostly on postwar race relations and politics: "Rebuilding was made hard due to the fact that slaves were now free and became economic competitors with poor whites especially, . . . furthermore, political corruption in the South was a huge problem, as was the leniency of the federal government toward readmitting southern states to the Union." She then read historian David Blight's response that focused largely on taxation:

> Taxation was a huge problem. It's not the most exciting subject in history to some people, but think about it. It was a huge problem in the Reconstruction states. How do you fund public facilities? How do you fund the public school? How do you build a hospital? How do you fund the dredging of a river? How do you rebuild Charleston, South Carolina? How do you rebuild Richmond? Where would the money come from? What do you tax? Do you tax land? Do you tax livestock? You can't tax slaves anymore because they don't exist. Who gets taxed, at what level? So they're debating public policy of the most important kind. They're debating the establishment of new

roads. They're debating the nature of elections. They're debating redistricting of states. In the old days, the districts of a state were gerrymandered by the planter class, so that basically the states were controlled by planters . . . from those regions.

This student then compared her response to Blight's and found the similarities and differences. She came to the conclusion that many factors, not just race relations and politics, made rebuilding hard and that a host of other factors, more than could probably be explained, contributed to the hardship. This particular student ended up crafting a historical narrative on the economics of racism, something that I thought was pretty neat.

Another student pursued the question "Did northerners realize how bad conditions were down South?" She was very proud that her response mirrored historian David Blight's. This student had stated that this was the "first time when Americans experienced a civil war, and so was finally catching up to the nations of Europe." Blight's response emphasized similar points:

> Like the destroyed abbeys of seventeenth-century England in the English civil war, which are still all over the English landscape . . . the South now was a landscape with ruins—ruined plantations. . . . America for the first time was a society with the experience of all-out war, that had given them ruins.

Although Blight's response is much more sophisticated, one can see that this was an empowering experience for the student. This particular student exclaimed, "Wow, I feel pretty smart that I was able to figure that one out!"

Consequently, when the students were given the opportunity to see models of how historians questioned, interpreted, reflected upon, and analyzed the same documents that they had two days prior, a powerful and profound learning experience occurred. Many students felt validated and proud of their insights into the past. I heard one student say, "Hey, these people aren't that smart. . . . I figured out the same thing!" Another student commented, "Wow, I never thought history was so complicated." Although it was not my intent to have my students disparage historians' intelligence, I was pleased to see that they were no longer seeing an insurmountable gulf between how historians make sense of the world and how they do. This exercise proved to be an excellent confidence builder.

Days 4–6: The Art of Writing History

On the last three days of the unit, I moved from more teacher-directed activities to more student-directed ones. During this time, the students drafted their own narratives of the Reconstruction era. They each crafted their own big idea statements and supported them with evidence researched throughout the two weeks.

I introduced this task by having the students brainstorm questions left unanswered about the era. I encouraged them to explore topics and ask questions based on information we had studied in class. Among the questions created by the students were:

How were Native Americans affected by the war?

How did westerners participate in the war; how were they affected by postwar policies?

Did the negatives of Reconstruction outweigh the positives?

How did women feel about the race for equality and the passage of the Fifteenth Amendment?

What role, if any, did religion play in the acquisition of black rights?

Asking my students to translate their questions into big ideas was an effort to get them thinking outside the box about what they already knew; it was an exercise in reflective practice. I did not want my students to be confined to looking for right or wrong answers, so as they started drafting their big ideas, I encouraged them to think of questions that they considered thought provoking and allowed them to formulate their own interpretations of them. I reminded them to think back to the big ideas we had used so far this year. For example, when studying Jacksonian democracy, our big idea was "Andrew Jackson: King or Common Man?" When we studied the war with Mexico, the big idea was "Manifest Destiny: God's Creed or America's Greed?" Many but not all students engaged in the task eagerly.

Some students quickly picked up on the task/challenge at hand. In short order, they came up with a range of big idea questions and statements:

- Reconstruction: Domestic terrorism: A war on minorities?
- All wars are fought over money.
- Reconstruction was a national disgrace.
- Reconstruction was a radical and noble attempt to establish an interracial democracy.
- Radical Reconstruction was not radical at all.
- The Constitution: Do the rules still apply when the nation's at war?
- Loss of the cash crop equaled the loss of the South.
- Silence is acquiescence: The federal government and the KKK.

Many of their questions/statements were open-ended, thoughtful, insightful, and relevant. They were thought provoking and perceptive. They helped me to assess what each student knew and understood about the topics researched.

After brainstorming these big ideas, I asked my students to reflect upon their interpretations of the primary source document research, their "Interview with a Historian" worksheet, and the "Compare/Contrast" task. With their big ideas in hand, students sketched a sample thesis statement in an attempt to actually answer their questions. For example, one student brainstormed the big idea question: "North vs. South: A struggle in ideology?" His thesis statement was "The North and the South were in an ideological struggle after the war had ended, with the North trying to 'modernize' the views of the South and the South trying desperately to redeem its culture." Another student's big idea was "Women: The weaker sex of the Reconstruction era." Her thesis statement was "Despite the U.S. government's attempt to keep women subservient to men after the Civil War, women were in fact gaining more prominence and importance in American society."

As the students worked on their big ideas and thesis statements, I reminded them that a historian's job is to draw on primary and secondary sources, either by quoting or paraphrasing, in order to support the claims that they are making or to challenge or supplement the interpretations that other historians have offered.

Some students showed little evidence of excitement as they engaged in this inquiry-oriented endeavor, and there were a few more groans and moans than I had anticipated. When I asked them what the problem was, a few stated, "This is just really hard work" and "We never had to do this before." A few even wanted to know, "Is this on the final exam?" and even "Why can't you just tell us what to write or what we need to know?" It was really hard for some students to see the difference between talking about a topic (i.e., knowing what happened) and making an argument (i.e., actually understanding what happened and why). But when the students got to the task of actually writing their histories, a degree of engagement and sophistication emerged that eclipsed my expectations. The ownership piece really hooked many into the process. Legitimizing their reasoning proved invaluable.

After the students wrote their narratives, we had a discussion about the following questions: What if students at school were taught only one point of view about the past? What might happen if freedom of opinion/expression did not exist? How do one's personal beliefs influence one's historical interpretations? Did your personal convictions/opinions influence the argument you created? The students' reactions were noteworthy. I was pleased to hear that many students understood the importance of assessing point of view and hence found relevance among the past week's tasks. I was impressed that many students were able to figure out that who one is as a person affects one's perspective as an author, that the persona—male or female, African American or Latino, northerner or southerner—influences our interpretations of the past. The students seemed to embrace these ideas. Among their comments were:

> "If there was no opinion allowed, history couldn't be written; it would just be a list of names and dates."

"One would not be able to open one's mind and craft one's own educated opinion, or make sense of the past."

"Everyone would be forced to think the same thing so we would only see history through the eyes of one group of people. . . . We wouldn't truly understand what history is all about."

"Absolutely, where you live affects your beliefs, as does your social class and race."

"Since I am a girl, I chose to research more about women's roles in the war. . . . I know they had to do something more than be nurses on the battlefields."

"If we were only taught one point of view, history would be boring; I wouldn't feel connected to it at all. I don't think I could empathize, probably wouldn't care because I couldn't relate."

After listening to these points, I articulated back to the students explicitly what skills they had just mastered. They were excited to hear that they were capable of interpreting primary, secondary, and tertiary documents, analyzing these writings, synthesizing information, decoding vocabulary, comparing and contrasting historical schools of thought, drafting thesis statements, and crafting unique historical narratives. After two weeks of hard work, most of the students felt proud of their accomplishments. One student stated, "This was the hardest thing I've done in school all year."

I then discussed with the students the purpose and importance of taking ownership of their learning. The quality of the dialogue was dynamic and quite lively, and the students expressed mixed emotions: They showed signs of gratitude for learning these skills but resentment because it took many of them eleven years to figure it out. Their responses were as enlightening as they were telling:

"How come we were never taught this stuff before in our other social studies classes? The classes would have been way more interesting."

"If history is all about interpretation, then how do we really know what happened in the past? Were we lied to?"

"I never knew that studying history was so complicated. I had no idea that people actually spent a lot of time thinking and analyzing the facts behind events. I didn't know it was so biased."

"Doing all of this stuff was hard work, but I learned that it is impossible to not think hard about the facts if you want to present a logical argument."

ASSESSMENT: A LESSON IN KNOWING VS. UNDERSTANDING

Later in the school year, we revisited some of the students' big idea questions and what they had learned about the nature of studying history. Many students were happy that their classmates deemed their theses valid. What I mean is that many of their theses proved to be legitimate or justifiable as we examined and studied additional documents, interpreted more historiography, and analyzed more primary and secondary sources throughout the school year. For example, when we studied Woodrow Wilson's presidency and previewed a few clips of the film *Birth of a Nation*, most of the students were able to predict and understand why Wilson, a southern Democrat, would praise the film. They were also able to understand, for example, why his record on race relations was not very progressive. One student exclaimed, "The only reason Wilson didn't support the NAACP and guys like Garvey was because he came from a family of rich southern aristocrats. There's no way he could have stayed in office if he made the southern states mad." Later still, when we watched clips of the PBS series *Eyes on the Prize* and previewed scenes from the segment on the murder of Emmitt Till, many students were able to predict and explain why many Americans who viewed the news coverage on TV would be horrified by the brutality of the South. As they noted, this was the first time many were exposed to such a different way of life, the southern perspective on race relations. One student noted, "My gosh that was only sixty years ago—my grandma is sixty—I can't believe southerners were still so backwards! No wonder the federal government started to pass laws to force the South to change its ways. It's all such a shame!"

Other students, however, were not too happy with their Reconstruction narratives. They were not happy with the quality of their research, their ability to think critically about the material, or their ability to question what they read. For example, one student said, "Oh, now I get it. When I wrote my essay on Reconstruction, I should've proven that Reconstruction wasn't all it was cracked up to be. I guess it really wasn't that effective in granting African Americans equality since America appeared to be more racist in 1920 than it did in 1860." Another student stated, "When I tried to prove in my thesis 'Silence is acquiescence: The federal government and the KKK,' I should've done more research about the future of race relations in the South in particular. . . . I could've included more positive stuff in my reflection, like how writers like Ida Tarbell opened people's eyes to the problem and how organizers like A. Phillip Randolph fought to end Jim Crow in the nation. Too bad I focused too much on the negatives."

Although the students were expressing doubts about their work, I took this as a sign that their ability to question what they thought they knew improved as the year progressed. The students who realized that they had come up short on the first try were really demonstrating that they gained an appreciation of historians' work. The key point here is that we teachers cannot expect students to get this stuff the first time through. It is hard for students (and adults) to know or identify what they do not know or what they want to know more about. That said, this chapter suggests that students will not automatically take the low road; they not only will rise to the challenges you put in front of them but also will be self-reflective and embrace them.

CONCLUSION

What is most fascinating about teaching historical inquiry is the development of skills that students master as they progress throughout the school year. It is fascinating to see that, by about mid-January, most students begin to realize history is less about recalling and memorizing facts and events and is more about discovering the big ideas. The fact that students progress tremendously in terms of how they make sense of historical documents, how they begin to craft original explanations for events, and how they use facts and evidence to support their interpretations is astounding. It is the use of big ideas as frameworks of understanding that guided my students to these realizations. Doing so provided support for students' conceptual understanding of the content; it helped them learn to problem solve. As teachers, we need to engage our students, we need to make them feel as though they have a voice in studying our nation's past, and we need to help them become active participants in investigating our history.

Empowering students to work as historians proved to be a profound learning experience. By my relinquishing some control, students had the opportunity to brainstorm questions, craft arguments, construct thesis statements, support them with evidence, and develop unique secondary sources which in turn enhanced student understanding. As I undertook the challenge of giving up some control in the classroom, I learned to trust my students' intellect and their ability to think and be creative. For when students know that you trust them, most will actually want to work hard for you, to produce, to showcase their knowledge and talents. By not trusting students' ability and capability and by not giving up some control in the classroom, we are underestimating these students. Overall, teaching the students the "what ifs," having them be active and engaged, and having them challenge what they learned about the Civil War and Reconstruction era proved to be a rewarding, rigorous, and viable way for them to learn about history.

APPENDIX A: SOURCE MATERIALS FOR THE READING FOR MEANING ACTIVITY

- Excerpts from the Civil Rights Act of 1866.
- The Civil Rights Act of 1875.

- Excerpt from Dorothy Sterling, ed., *Trouble They Seen: The Story of Reconstruction in the Words of African Americans*. New York: Da Capo, 1994.
- Excerpt from John Hope Franklin, ed., *Reminiscences of an Active Life: The Autobiography of John Roy Lynch*. Chicago: University of Chicago Press, 1970.
- Excerpt from Final Report to the South Carolina House, 1874.
- Journal of the House of Representatives of the State of South Carolina, for the Regular Session of 1874–1874 (Columbia, 1874), 549–553. Reprinted in William Loren Katz, *Eyewitness*. New York: Simon and Schuster, 1995.
- Excerpt from Senate Report 693, 46th Congress, 2nd Session (1880). Reprinted in Sterling, *The Trouble They Seen*.
- Excerpt from Benjamin Morgan Palmer, Thanksgiving Sermon, Delivered at the First Presbyterian Church, New Orleans, on Thursday, December 29, 1860. New York: G. F. Hesbit, 1860.
- Excerpts from Testimony of B. W. Marston Re: The Coushatta Affair. House Reports, 44th Congress, 1st Session, No. 816, 645–727.
- Excerpt from Testimony Taken by the Joint Select Committee to Inquire into the Condition of Affairs in the Late Insurrectionary States (Washington, 1872). Reprinted in Sterling, *The Trouble They Seen*.

APPENDIX B: QUESTIONS/THESES FOR THE PRIOR KNOWLEDGE ACQUISITION ACTIVITY

- Myth or reality: Yankees and blacks conspired to exploit the South after the war.
- Myth or reality: The Klan was a small group of renegades from southern society's fringes.
- Myth or reality: Confederate soldiers were heroes because their cause was noble.
- Myth or reality: The black legislators elected during Reconstruction were all corrupt.

- Myth or reality: Everyone in the South was happy before the war.
- How does the Reconstruction era civil rights debate connect to twentieth- and twenty-first-century civil rights movements?
- How was learning to read connected to the end of slavery? How challenging was it for a former slave to become literate and embrace citizenship?
- How did southern resistance to black freedom play out after the Civil War?
- Compare and contrast Lincoln's and Johnson's plans for Reconstruction. How did Congress react to both?
- How "radical" were the Radical Republicans?
- Assess the effectiveness of the Black Codes.
- Was the Fourteenth Amendment effective in granting African Americans due process?
- Was military reconstruction effective?
- What were the southern state governments' problems, achievements, and weaknesses?
- Did northern whites have any business getting involved in the politics of the New South?
- Assess women's reactions to the Reconstruction amendments.
- How was the solid South "redeemed" after the war?
- How did most nineteenth-century Americans view racial equality?
- What did northerners think about black civil rights during Reconstruction?
- What were the two major political parties' positions on black civil rights at the time?
- What did the nineteenth-century civil rights legislation try to accomplish?
- What kind of destruction did the South suffer?
- How did the nation approach the process of rebuilding? How did philosophies about rebuilding differ? In practice, what made rebuilding so hard?
- How was learning to read connected to the end of slavery?

- Did former slaves need to become educated to gain political power? Was there government support for educating ex-slaves? Could former slaves educate themselves on their own initiative? How challenging was it for a former slave to become literate and embrace citizenship?
- How did landowners and freedmen resolve their differences over labor issues?
- Why did many southern blacks stay on the land where they had been slaves? How did the idea of sharecropping originate? Could freed slaves actually succeed as sharecroppers? How did these changes in black labor affect white workers?
- How did southern resistance to black freedom play out after the Civil War? What did southern whites think about sharing political power with their former slaves?
- What was the Ku Klux Klan? Were blacks the Klan's only targets? What kind of thinking lay behind Klan actions? Did other southern whites take a stand against the violence? Did retaliatory violence exist?
- How did groups like the Klan justify their violent acts? Did such violence go unchecked?

9

BIG IDEAS AND AMBITIOUS TEACHING: A CROSS-CASE ANALYSIS

Jill M. Gradwell and S. G. Grant

Ambitious teaching offers no nirvana; it can be challenging, frustrating, and complex. But as the teacher-authored chapters in this book attest, teaching with big ideas presents the kind of ambitious teaching and learning opportunities to which teachers say they aspire. Key to such teaching are three sets of knowledge: knowledge of the subject matter, knowledge of the students one is teaching, and knowledge of the teaching context. In the first section of this chapter, we describe how the teacher-authors employ these different kinds of knowledge in ways that provide robust learning opportunities for their students. In the second part of the chapter, we turn our attention to the problems and possibilities these teachers encountered along the road to ambitious teaching.

THE NECESSARY KNOWLEDGE: SUBJECT MATTER, STUDENTS, AND CONTEXT

In chapter 1, we argued that knowledge of subject matter, students, and context, individually and together, anchors the construct of ambitious teaching. Ambitious teachers understand their subject matter well and see the promise it holds for enriching their students' lives. They also know their students well—which includes understanding the kinds of lives their students lead and how these youngsters think about and perceive the world—and have high expectations for them. Finally, ambitious teachers know how to create the necessary space for themselves and their students in environments in which others, like their principals or colleagues, may not appreciate their efforts. Ambitious teaching, then, is not so much about the teaching strategies a teacher employs but rather is what a teacher knows and how she or he engages with ideas, students, and the respective teaching context.

Knowledge of Subject Matter

New York State has a long history of creating state-level content curricula. These curricula typically are highly specific and unwieldy (e.g., the grade 11 U.S. history curriculum is twenty-two single-spaced pages). Advanced Placement (AP) courses offer similarly dense curricula. Rather than adopt a defensive strategy (McNeil, 2000) and give every idea an equal measure of attention, ambitious teachers well know the ideas that resonate within their fields. These teachers' strong content knowledge enables them to put big ideas in front of students when the state curriculum, state tests, and their colleagues do not. Some of those ideas are substantive or content centered; others focus on methodological issues.

Joseph Karb and Andrew Beiter, two middle school teachers from a rural school district, initially looked to the state curriculum for guidance about teaching the Holocaust. What they found is that the Holocaust receives only passing notice—a short, twenty-five-word listing of related topics and themes. They understood that a curriculum document cannot cover every issue in depth, but they worried that teachers may interpret the cursory reference as license to skim over the Holocaust:

> This document is not designed to be all inclusive, but it seems strange to us that an event which can teach students so much about life is given only cursory attention. This brief mention—coupled with the pressure of the state assessment—results in many teachers spending less than one day on the Holocaust in their race to cover everything else.

Unlike many other teachers, Karb and Beiter chose otherwise, dedicating two weeks of class time to the Holocaust and recent genocides. They note that some teachers find it hard to justify such use of time, given that there may only be one question on the state exam. They believe, however, that "teachers do have a responsibility to be more than assessment robots and to teach lessons that will impact students' views of the world." Their beliefs about history and the better understanding of it emphasize the notion of depth over breadth, an approach encouraged by education reformers (Wiggins & McTighe, 1998) and adopted by other ambitious-minded teachers (Kelly & VanSledright, 2005).

Michael Meyer, a teacher from a second-ring, affluent school district, also looked to the state curriculum for direction when he tried to develop a unit about early Africa. Finding little there, he looked at past New York State global history and geography exam questions. He concluded that the same couple of questions appeared year after year. Disappointed, he wondered about the mixed messages that seemed inherent in the state curriculum and assessment approaches:

> I found it interesting that the state asked a question pointing out that there were civilizations before the Europeans arrived but did not ask about those civilizations. I also thought it was unfortunate that the area of the world about which my students probably knew the least required me to teach the least about it. I started to feel that it was wrong to send the message to the students that Africa doesn't matter.

Still not satisfied, he approached some of his department colleagues only to find they spent very little time on Africa. In effect, their units boiled down to content coverage of past state exam questions. This approach is not unusual (Gerwin & Visone, 2006), but it lies some distance from the approach taken by ambitious teachers.

Like Karb and Beiter, Meyer uses his strong understanding of the content to drive his teaching. He understands that Africa has played a dynamic role throughout history, that

> the case of Africa shows where race and power can affect history and how that flawed history can continue to affect modern views of race and power; history and racism are historically connected and constructed; to address modern problems, it can be instructive to examine where they came from.

Given his sophisticated understanding of Africa's past and present history, Meyer chose to frame his unit around the big idea question "Why don't we know anything about Africa?" hoping to give his students a fresh angle on an often-neglected part of the world.

Mary Beth Bruce, a teacher from a first-ring suburb, teaches an Advanced Placement American history course. Her background as a history major influences her decisions about the content she emphasizes in her classes. She also uses her knowledge of history as a discipline to help students understand the methodology of history, that is, how history is constructed:

> I believed it was important to teach kids how history is constructed and interpreted. I wanted kids to learn more than the chronology and facts of the past and the epic travels of our Founding Fathers and Mothers. I wanted them to "do" history, to analyze documents from the past, to determine their authenticity, and to formulate their own views about events.

Karb, Beiter, Meyer, and Bruce all make instructional choices based on a number of factors, one being their sophisticated understanding of history. Although strong disciplinary knowledge alone does not predict an ambitious learning environment, it does play a major role (Grant, 2003; Wineburg & Wilson, 1991; Yeager & Davis, 1996).

In a variation on the theme, Tricia Davis, an experienced inner-city charter school teacher, uses her knowledge of the subject matter not only to frame her units around big ideas but also to make different instructional choices. She believes that students can learn about history through a variety of means, especially writing: "I have always believed that students could learn more about historical content through the process of writing. Writing is part of the construction of knowledge to be used in conjunction with active shared learning experiences in the classroom." When developing her units of study, she reviews the state curriculum and then crafts a list of big ideas to build her lessons and assessments around. In her Encounter unit, for example, Davis created a series of writing tasks from the various viewpoints of the historical actors of the time, for she believes that the "ability to see history through the eyes of the people involved is an important skill in thinking historically." Rather than let the state curriculum or state testing format drive her assessment choices in the classroom, she relies on her knowledge of the subject matter and how it can best be translated for her students' understanding.

The teachers profiled above, like the others in this project, looked for guidance from numerous sources to determine how they would design their lessons and units. But instead of following the heading outlines in the state curriculum, the most often asked questions on the state exam, or the stock references of their peers, these teachers, like Paula Maron in Libresco's (2005) study, choose to structure their academic units around open-ended questions or big ideas. In each instance, they used their content-knowledge backgrounds to seize control of the curriculum. They know well the state polices and the local practices, but they also know that they can manipulate the curriculum to best serve their pedagogical needs.

Knowledge of Learners

Ambitious teachers know their subject matter well, but they also know well the students who attend their classes. Such teachers realize that, although there are general patterns to student interests and behaviors, their particular students often bring local patterns and idiosyncrasies to bear. Recognizing the unique qualities their respective students possess and making pedagogical choices to complement those qualities are key components to ambitious teaching. The teachers in this group reach out to their students through many means, be it by connecting history to students' everyday lives, linking past events to present-day circumstances, or focusing on everyday peoples' lives of the past.

Sarah Foels, for example, linked students' everyday life experiences to the historical conflict around slavery in the United States. A grade 8 teacher in a second-ring suburban district, Foels noticed that her students struggled when she had them analyze documents to determine the pros and cons of slavery. Attributing this difficulty to their sense of presentism and inability to put documents in their appropriate historical context, she soon realized that she had to find a way to help her students consider why there were multiple viewpoints of slavery—the larger goal of the lesson. To do so, she structured her next lesson around a dilemma her students were likely to have encountered in their everyday lives:

> I decided that students would have an easier time connecting to the overarching goal of the lesson if I first posed the following personal questions at the beginning of class: "Think of an argument that you had with someone. What reasons did you give to support your ideas? What reasons did he or she give to support his or her ideas? Who was 'right' and who was 'wrong'? Explain."

After some discussion, her students came to understand that, in any argument, there are various sides. She then extended her question, asking her students to consider if slavery was a necessary evil or just plain evil. She found that her students were better equipped to answer the question from the various viewpoints of the historical actors of the time. She explained that students now seemed capable of expressing more varied and complex positions: "It seemed as though my students were beginning to see that perspectives on an issue changed depending on the individual person."

Foels's use of metaphors and analogies is similar to that of Elizabeth Jensen, the American history teacher in Wineburg and Wilson's

(1991) study of the role strong subject knowledge of teachers plays in their classrooms. Jensen, like Foels, understood that abstract ideas can intimidate students and that framing historical questions around ideas with which students have experience can bridge the gaps in their knowledge and understanding.

Julie Doyle, a global history teacher from a rural school district, also focused on issues that resonate with her particular students as a way to frame her units. When she developed her Age of Imperialism unit, she tapped into her students' sense of fairness: "I believed it was important to develop a big idea that appealed to their strong sense of justice and offered them the opportunity to evaluate policies from multiple perspectives." She framed the lessons around a central question: "Does imperialism help or hurt native people?" Believing that her students become easily confused when vast global topics are presented in a chronological format, she instead presented her unit based on an open-ended, moral framework. In doing so, she hoped her students would be more apt to "view the world with a smart, critical lens." Teachers who, like Doyle, refine their teaching methods and incorporate more open-ended questioning techniques report both their excitement and delight with the seeming improvement in their students' historical understanding (Bain, 2000). However, ambitious teachers also know there is still room for growth and that it is likely not all students reach the same complex historical awareness.

Rookie, urban grade 8 teacher Megan Sampson also wanted to help her students connect to history, and she did so by tracing the chronological development of modern-day problems. Enthusiastically, she framed her course around big ideas in hopes that "students would find more success with the content if I could help them relate to it." She believed that "if I could make world history relevant to them and show them that the struggles of the past are the same as the struggles today, they would find that information much easier to recall and use." For example, she linked the current issue of religious conflict to its historic roots as a way to reach her students. The goal she defined was "to show them that the events of the past and the events of the present are rooted in current ideas and emotions."

Barton and Levstik (2004) might argue that Sampson is taking on an analytic stance to teaching history. Perhaps so. But she does it less as a way to create little historians than as a way to help her students see their way into the past through their lived experiences. In doing so, she is helping her students prepare to be contributing citizens in a pluralist democracy.

Another way some of the teacher-authors tried to relate history to their students was through the personal stories of those who lived during major historical eras. One of Karb and Beiter's goals for their big idea unit was to foster perspective-taking among their students about an extremely sensitive and horrifying topic, the Holocaust. To help students understand the sheer numbers of victims, they focused on individual victims' stories: "To teach the numbers of the Holocaust, we had to scale that big number down to one—in other words, *one* student relating to *one* victim, thus making the incomprehensible tangible." The payoff, they report, was immediate and intense: "The students reacted in serious and somber ways, seeming to internalize the power of the activity. 'What we did today made me see that they were people too,' said a student."

By constructing the activity in this fashion, Karb and Beiter laid the psychological framework for students to care about the Holocaust. Numerous studies (Brophy & VanSledright, 1997; Kohlmeier, 2005; Levstik & Groth, 2002) support their inclination that students are especially interested in individuals from the past and how they constructed their lives, even those connected to the Holocaust (Schweber, 2003).

Ambitious teachers understand that there are no generic students. Constructing powerful teaching units, then, means knowing how their students make sense of the world. For when students can connect to the past, they are more likely to remember it and use it in their everyday lives (Gradwell, 2006; Grant, 2003).

Knowledge of Context

Not only do ambitious teachers have a strong understanding of the content and their students, but they also need to find ways to navigate the settings they are in to provide those spaces for their students to thrive. Karb and Beiter summarize the several contextual factors they must negotiate daily: "We teach, after all, in an imperfect world that is rife with obstacles, roadblocks, and constraints. Standardized assessments, teacher in-service days, and snow days all chip away at the time we have with our students." Instead of letting these possible barriers to rich instruction get in the way of their teaching, they look past them to better reach their students: "Our intent is not to pretend that these obstacles don't exist, but instead to acknowledge, understand, and even embrace them as a way of advancing our profession."

That teachers work within a nested set of contexts proves challenging on multiple levels. Ambitious teachers realize, however, that the people and policies surrounding them may offer as many problems as possibilities for rich teaching and learning. The possibilities, manifest in the instructional practices of the teacher-authors represented in this book, have taken root in soil that was not always fertile. Each teacher had to negotiate a set of challenges from without and from within, any of which could have caused him or her to abandon the effort.

The challenges related to the contextual environment each teacher faced varied, but they can be grouped under two general categories—lack of experience working with inclusion and challenging students, and working in an overly test-oriented school climate.

When Sarah Foels first learned she was going to be taking on a section of inclusion students, she doubted her students' abilities and questioned her own ability as a teacher. She asked herself several questions: "How were students with disabilities going to handle generalizations and abstract ideas?" and "How was I going to manage such a big class and still accomplish what I had tried out the year before?" Later, as she introduced big ideas to her inclusion students, she learned that they are a powerful intervention with all groups of students:

Most importantly, I realized that no one was left out of the learning experience. Both regular education and special education students were actively participating in our more student-centered class. The units seemed to help students at a variety of academic levels understand the general themes that appear in U.S. history and made it easier for them to chunk specific details together to better memorize facts for the assessment.

Though Foels struggled in developing big ideas across all her units for all her students, she soon saw the payoff in terms of active student engagement and stronger understanding of history. She learned what Sarah Cooper, the teacher in Gradwell's (2006) study, sensed about students with diverse academic abilities. In Cooper's wildly diverse class of grade 8 students, equal thirds identified as gifted, regular education, and special education. Cooper did not let the class make-up determine how she structured her course or dictate the types of materials she used with the students. In the end, Cooper, like Foels, learned that all her students performed well on class assignments and state assessments.

A veteran grade 10 teacher, Tricia Davis faced a different contextual concern: making the transition from working with one population of students to another. After teaching several years in parochial and suburban schools, she took a position in a charter school to work with an inner-city student population that typically has a high drop-out rate. Although she was not completely satisfied with her teaching of writing skills in previous teaching jobs, she was comforted with the knowledge that, by having her students repeatedly practice writing past state essay prompts, they would do fine on the state exam. As she points out, however, her previous practices "were not going to fly" with her new students. She wondered if she could cover the requisite history content and teach her students to write well.

To meet the challenge, Davis moved away from modeling her assessments on the state exam format and instead spent more time teaching her students how to respond to more interesting historical questions. The result: she believes she "took a leap of faith," and that "it has borne fruit" in the form of good student writing.

In one way or another, each of the teacher-authors in this book faced the New York State exams and Advanced Placement exams as a contextual issue. None was cowed into the kind of pedantic teaching that some researchers have reported (McNeil, 2000; Vogler, 2006). Instead, each found that using big ideas and a more ambitious teaching approach proved helpful in dealing with the potential constraint those standardized tests represent.

Michael Meyer's context demonstrates an interesting variation on the typical dilemma teachers confront regarding state-level testing. Where most teachers worry about their students passing the exams, Meyer and his colleagues faced a different challenge: their students routinely pass the state exam, so the pressure is to pass at the mastery level:

> I am aware that in many school districts the main concern is just to get students to *pass* the tests. In our school and community, it is *assumed* that we will get all the kids to pass the tests, that is, to achieve a score of 65 or above. So for us, the goal is to get as many students as possible to achieve a score of 85 or above.

New York State policymakers set the pass rate at 65 out of 100; the mastery mark is 85. Parents, community members, and administrators in the district in which Meyer teaches demand more than students merely passing the state exams. As Meyer puts it, "the pressure isn't for achieving passing scores; it is for excelling." In response, many of his colleagues have turned their classrooms into year-long test preparation programs. Meyer resists that practice, in large part because he thinks the big idea approach he uses more fully engages his students. But he can also resist his colleagues' practices because his students score as well as or better than their students do. Some of his peers may grumble at his methods, but they cannot argue with his success.

In most of the cases in this book, the teacher-authors are able to navigate successfully around the contextual barriers that confront them. Sampson's case is one that offers a cautionary tale. After Sampson had prepared her students for the state competency test, the school administrator decided the students would instead take the more rigorous Regents exam. The students, disheartened by the change of plan, failed the exam. Thus, the decisions of others can dramatically and negatively affect a teacher's most ambitious efforts.

Being ambitious means knowing one's content knowledge, presenting it in ways that make sense for students, and doing so despite less than favorable teaching environments. The teachers in this book possess such knowledge, and their specific cases show what is possible in an age of accountability. Other than being ambitious, they share another practice—the use of big ideas to teach history. In the next section, we present some of the issues, dilemmas, and successes these teachers had when teaching history with big ideas.

TEACHING HISTORY WITH BIG IDEAS: PROBLEMS AND POSSIBILITIES

In the last section, we focused on the ambitious practices of the teacher-authors as they pertain to knowledge of subject matter, students, and context. In this section, we describe both the problems and possibilities for teaching history with big ideas. Each teacher faced her or his own set of dilemmas in developing and enacting big ideas in their respective classrooms. However, some common problems arose that can be grouped under four general categories— difficulties in grasping the big idea concept, unsupportive school contexts for teaching with big ideas, lack of student familiarity with learning history through big ideas, and uncertainty about knowing what students know. With problems, however, come possibilities. And in the case of big idea teaching, those opportunities include the ability to engage all students' ideas and imaginations, to help students make authentic connections to historical actors and events, and to elevate students' voices in classroom activities. We argue, as the teachers do, that the potential for big idea teaching clearly outweighs the associated problems.

The Challenge of Teaching with Big Ideas

Mary Beth Bruce noted that although she had encountered big ideas in her history classes, she found it difficult to appreciate the pedagogical nature of the construct when encountering it in her social studies methods class: "To be honest, I didn't get it at all at first and was actually quite hesitant to utilize and implement this pedagogical strategy. I originally perceived the big ideas as a catchphrase or fancy title for a unit; the concept just didn't quite click." Other teachers, like Michael Meyer, thought they understood the construct but concluded that it was just another "grad school" idea that might or might not have any salience for actual classroom practice.

Still other teachers questioned their ability to translate big idea teaching that had worked in one school context into another. For example, Sarah Foels found that after some initial resistance, her honors-level students embraced the notion of big historical ideas. Yet when she was assigned to a new class with inclusion students, her confidence waned. She wanted to use big ideas to orient her teaching lessons and units, but she worried that doing so might leave some students confused:

> When I first switched from teaching my small class of honors students to teaching an inclusion class with twice as many students and a consultant teacher during my second year, I was convinced that my use of big ideas and hands-on activities would no longer be feasible on such a frequent basis.

Regardless of their initial hesitance to use big ideas to teach history, each of the teacher-authors came to the same conclusion: big idea teaching benefited their struggling students as much as and sometimes more than their advanced students. This realization can come hard for many teachers, however, largely because the prevailing wisdom is that ambitious teaching and learning are the province of high-ability students. Those deemed less capable are often treated to mind-numbing approaches that neither teach them the facts nor persuade them that history is worth examining. Although seemingly counterintuitive to many teachers, the research evidence is quite clear: higher rather than lower expectations and more rather than less challenging instruction yield improved student performance (Avery, 1999; Smith & Niemi, 2001; Stevenson, 1990). The teachers represented in this book may have struggled in crafting big ideas, but they persisted, and in doing so, they advantaged all of their students.

Unsupportive School Contexts for Teaching with Big Ideas

That these teachers persisted and for the most part succeeded could not have been guaranteed. Good teaching is a complex activity and can go off track for any number of reasons. One of those reasons is the powerful influence of school contexts and peer interactions. Sometimes those factors were enabling. At other times, however, school administrators and fellow teachers acted in ways that undercut the teacher-authors' best intentions and practices.

It will surprise few observers to learn that several of the teachers reported a pressure to tailor their teaching to state-level history tests. New York State has a long history of providing state-sanctioned curricula and mandating fairly rigorous standardized tests.[1] As the stakes attached to those exams have been ratcheted upward (Grant, 2006), teachers increasingly hear implicit and explicit messages that reduce to "Teach to the test."

Before she moved to her current school site, Tricia Davis and her colleagues in a first-ring Buffalo suburb were pushed to factor state tests into their instructional practices:

> The writing assessments that entered my grade book were based on writing prompts that mirrored the Regents exam prompts as closely as possible. Such was the explicitly stated mandate from my public school administrators. As I recall it, my department chair said (quoting the assistant superintendent for curriculum), "All assessments must parallel New York State Regents exams." So I, along with all my colleagues in the social studies department, used state prompts.

Mary Beth Bruce, who teaches in a first-ring suburb, also describes the district administrators' emphasis on test results. At the end of the school year, teachers are required to participate in a "data day" where they are presented with detailed analyses of their students' performances on the state exam. Bruce feels that the school district may support teaching history with big ideas, but "on the last day of school, the only things celebrated are Regents exam results." Although Michael Meyer teaches in a much more affluent community, he describes a similar sentiment being presented by his principal: "Just so there is no confusion about whether or not you should be teaching to the tests, let me be clear: teach to the test—it is how you will be evaluated."

Davis, Bruce, and Meyer, together with most of the teacher-authors in this book, found ways to mitigate the deleterious effects of state testing as interpreted by school administrators. As a rookie teacher in a Buffalo charter school, however, Megan Sampson experienced a much more problematic school context. One of her teaching assignments was to work with a small group of students who had previously failed the grade 10 Regents test in global history and geography. Her charge was to prepare the students to take the Regents Competency Test (RCT) version of the global history exam.[2] Sampson rejected the idea of presenting a facts-only curriculum in favor of one based on big ideas. Reluctant to commit themselves at first, her students soon embraced the approach and seemed excited to take the RCT. Days before they were scheduled to take the exam, however, Sampson learned along with her students that they would be taking the more challenging Regents test. The students were crestfallen: "They were upset and feeling defeated. They expressed anger that they were just being informed about taking the Regents exam. They said that they didn't think it was fair because they were not ready." Although Sampson tried to talk the students into rising to the challenge, the change had staggered them: "They were lost to me after this news. All the fear and doubt I had worked so hard to rid them of was back."

As heartbreaking as Sampson's story is, the notion that school administrators may not support teachers' more ambitious efforts is no particular surprise. Increasingly, administrators in high-stakes testing states are held responsible for students' exam scores. That they might become fixated on passing or on mastery rates makes sense even if the often implicit message of dumbing down the curriculum does not. Perhaps more discouraging, however, are the teachers who seem content to adopt and promote that implicit message, tailoring their content to frequently tested ideas and tailoring their instruction and assessments to practice-test questions (Vogler, 2006). The curriculum narrowing that a number of observers have noted (McNeil, 2000; Smith, 1991) is evident in Meyer's experience after he consulted the state curriculum and test:

> When I talked to some teachers about what the kids really needed to know about Africa, the first answer I got was "Nothing." As I pressed further, I got "Teach something about the Bantu migrations . . . they ask that every year." Then I got what turned out to be a similar response from two other teachers, one of whom said, "Let me put it this way, I am teaching and testing about Africa on Friday." This attitude was confirmed later in the year when I was walking through one of the teacher's classrooms. As he was putting up his overhead of notes about Africa, he said, "I have to apologize about this unit . . . it is a bit like a Hoover vacuum . . . it sucks."

Ambitious teachers understand that the adults around them may neither understand nor support their best instructional efforts (Grant, 2003, 2005). But they also know such understanding and support are not necessary. The decentralized nature of schooling (Cohen & Spillane, 1992) means that teachers hold considerable classroom autonomy. Moreover, as these teachers know, the psychic rewards of teaching (Lortie, 1975) come from students' eager and expansive responses and are what matter most.

Lack of Student Familiarity with Learning History with Big Ideas

As frustrating as the misunderstandings and lackadaisical support by one's peers and administrators can be, even more discouraging is the resistance students often display when confronted with more challenging teaching approaches. Most teachers assume that students will enthusiastically and immediately embrace rich instructional opportunities. After all, the standard student complaint of "This is so boring" suggests that a more engaging alternative is desired. As Dewey (1902/1969) pointed out, however, we get used to the chains we wear. Students accustomed to pedantic, easy schoolwork may whine about it, yet they may actually rebel when presented with more interesting but challenging tasks. Bizarre as this reaction sounds, it happens with sufficient regularity as to be recognized by most teachers.

That it happens is small consolation to those to whom it happens. Megan Sampson paints her experience in clear if plaintive fashion: "As the students came in, the first thing I encountered was skepticism and uncertainty. They accepted my approach to the course and were responsive to working with me, but the big ideas took them off guard." Sarah Foels's account of introducing big ideas to her students follows a similar trajectory. Her students reacted negatively to her attempts to frame her units and lessons around more complex ideas:

> There was a little bit of resistance at first because the regular education students did not know what to do with big ideas. When I asked them to consider broader analyses of topics in discussions and essays, they thought that I was looking for a specific answers and kept asking me whether or not they had the correct answers.

Though they resisted at first, both Sampson's and Foels's students eventually came around to embrace the big idea teaching their teachers offered. But teaching history with big ideas is no easy endeavor, and doing so with students unfamiliar with this type of approach is doubly difficult. To do so successfully, the teachers found that they had to help students negotiate the different kinds of questions and tasks and responsibilities demanded of them. That students invariably responded positively ought to give readers some sense of confidence that similar efforts could produce similar results. But Sampson's and Foels's early experiences serve as a useful cautionary tale: approach big idea teaching and learning with open eyes and a steady nerve.

Knowing What Students Know

The cautions the teacher-authors offer take at least one more form: the dilemma of knowing what students know. As most dilemmas are, this one turns out to be problematic on a number of levels (Baker, 1994; Grant, 2007; Nuthall & Alton-Lee, 1995; VanSledright, Kelly, & Meuwissen, 2006). Although teaching with big ideas helps teachers to focus the instructional intent of their units, questions about assessing students remain.

As part of his argument about the value teachers place on psychic rewards, Lortie (1975) describes the endemic uncertainty that arises about teachers' assessments of their students' learning. "Education is a tenuous, uncertain affair," he notes (p. 113). Lortie highlights the special dilemma teachers face in trying to assess their students' understandings: "Critical, recurrent problems remain unresolved in the daily work of teachers—uncertainty stalks as they try to determine whether they are influencing students" (p. 150).

Meyer nicely captures something of the range of anxiety and uncertainty that surrounds his sense of what his students learned:

> Although I can never be certain exactly what the kids have learned from the unit, I have taken their concluding answers to "Why don't we know anything about Africa?" and "Why does Africa matter?" as proof of some change. . . . [Still] I am sure that not all the students are getting it. In fact, I do admit that there are definitely those who don't or won't get it. One year, at least two students, in response to the question "Why does Africa matter?" simply wrote, "It doesn't."

Disappointing as such a response is, at least it is a response. Most every teacher knows the far more frustrating situation of putting forward a question and facing only a sea of blank expressions.

Tricia Davis encountered an unusual problem: students became too emotionally involved in their essay responses. Although this seems like a good problem to have, she points to the assessment difficulty that arose when some students "got wrapped up in the emotional content of their writing and ignored the major components of the task." Many teachers long for their students to find a personal connection to the past. Creating such connections may prove invaluable for classroom activities, but they can interfere with a teacher's judgment about what an invested student knows. Wrapped up in a personal narrative reaction, students may leave out key information that demonstrates an understanding of the event and thus may cast doubt on their competence. Davis may *know* that the students know the information, but if it is not represented, it is not assessable.

Sarah Foels points out one additional aspect of the assessment dilemma, that test scores may not rise even if engagement with historical ideas does:

> While our assessment scores did not change significantly from previous years, we recognized the importance of making history more meaningful and relevant to students. On an exit survey at the end of the year, most students reported that they felt they had learned to think about history more in my class, and they thought the themes were useful for organizing and discussing social studies concepts. Those comments were more important to me than any assessment scores could ever have been.

Although there seems to be some correlation between more challenging teaching approaches and higher standardized test scores (Smith & Niemi, 2001), there are no guarantees. Still, most teachers would accept the condition where student interest in history rises while test scores remain flat.

THE POSSIBILITIES FOR TEACHING WITH BIG IDEAS

Although the teacher-authors faced many obstacles to teaching with big ideas, they strongly believe the benefits for students outweigh any logistical, administrative, or contextual problems they encounter along the way. Specifically, they find that framing lessons and units around more authentic ideas engages their students in ways other approaches have not.

Megan Sampson captures the overall feeling of the teachers:

> The students started to think for themselves; they did not wait for me to tell them what to think. They told me stories from their own lives that related to topics of government, society, or economics; they talked about how topics of religion or politics related to their

beliefs and experiences. I could see that they were invested and interested in the material because they spoke about history being alive in their lives. They did not rely on guided worksheets on which all their answers were merely copied from a book. Their journal entries expressed their thoughts, prompted only by a question unlikely to be found in a textbook. Instead of sitting mindlessly and copying down notes from an overhead, they researched information on their own, asked questions, and found their own answers. They were active learners engaged in the material.

As Sampson explains, teaching with big ideas pushes students to become more active and engaged learners—no small feat since she was working with a group of students receiving remediation to pass the state exam. Using big ideas enables more students, like Sampson's, to participate more fully in the learning process. This was apparent when her students investigated the past on their own and asked questions of interest to them. Her students connected past events to the present day and voiced how history is "alive in their lives." Her experience with big ideas is not unique; all the teachers in this study conveyed similar accounts.

We argue that working with big ideas promotes richer instructional units leading to elevated student engagement with and involvement in their own learning. The teachers believe that they see more of their students participating in classroom activities, making strong connections to the discipline of history, and voicing their own understandings of the past.

More Students Participating in the Learning Process

One of the issues that most teachers wrestle with is how to meet the needs of all of their learners in heterogeneously grouped classrooms. The move to include more students in "regular" classes promotes an important goal: giving all students the opportunity to experience rich instruction. Yet even before the inclusion effort, many teachers struggled to engage all of their students. The teacher-authors in this book are no different. What they have found, however, is that teaching with big ideas offers a way for more students to be involved with their learning. Sampson put the matter succinctly: "I especially felt that this approach was what my struggling students needed. They needed to feel that history is tangible and approachable, and that they could be successful with the content."

As the teachers grew more accustomed to teaching with big ideas, and as they saw its success across diverse audiences, they continued retooling their units around questions that provoked student interest. Doing so, Sarah Foels realized, resulted in more entry points for students who were typically unresponsive: "After completing my first unit, and seeing that students were able to successfully demonstrate their understanding of the big idea, I was excited to develop more units." Although Foels was initially hesitant to teach history with big ideas to her inclusion students, she concluded that they benefited as much as her honors students, leading her to expand her use of big ideas.

Julie Doyle echoed this: "I have seen an increase in the number of engaged students, and that has inspired me to use this methodology more and more." Like Foels, Doyle saw that more of her students were involved in the learning process, and she therefore continued to devise units around big ideas.

Many teachers focus their attention on their instructional methods and give authority over the content to state and local curriculum guides (Cornbleth, 2002). Big idea teachers cede nothing. They understand two things about the relationship between content and instructional decisions. First, they know that the power of the ideas draws students into their lessons, so they transform the often staid representations of ideas from content guides into big ideas. Second, they realize that big idea teaching demands no particular set of instructional practices (Grant, 2003). Small-group projects, demonstrations, discussions, and even lectures are all appropriate. Teachers use the ideas and their instructional goals to determine the methods they use, not the reverse. Big idea teaching is about framing intellectually rich ideas into questions that students can embrace. When they do so, they find that normally reticent students join in.

Students Connect with History

One reason that teachers struggle to involve all their students is the challenge of helping students connect the past with their present lives (Grant, 2003). To offset this difficulty, the teachers in this book create big ideas that reflect their students' interests. As Sampson points out, "For me, teaching with big ideas meant making history real for my students." Making history real is an oft-stated teacher goal. The teacher-authors in this book discovered ways to reach that goal.

To help her students connect with the past, Sarah Foels eschews content coverage, focusing instead on units with broad, enduring themes. With a theme identified, she then uses open-ended questions, the elements of historical argument, and the opportunity to define one's own position to lure students in:

> Instead of focusing exclusively on the teaching of content, I had attempted to find a broader question or idea that students could connect with. By asking students to relate arguments in general to analyzing the validity of different historical arguments with respect to a specific topic, I had been able to make the content meaningful and open to evaluation. It seemed that the students had enjoyed answering an open question about the topic instead of simply memorizing and regurgitating information. I had not told them what to think but had given them ownership over their own knowledge and comprehension of the material.

When the teachers teach history through a big idea approach, they report that their students find history to be more accessible and meaningful to them. Foels senses that her students enjoyed responding to the open-ended, big idea questions. She attributes this response to them having "ownership over their own knowledge" rather than having their thinking controlled.

Still other teachers use current events to structure big ideas that they believe will engage their students' interest in the past. Sampson begins one unit with the big idea question "What makes a society stable and successful?" The lively class discussion that ensued focused on issues of overpopulation throughout the world today.

Sampson observed how the current events question "What makes a society stable and successful?" motivated students:

> One of my students came in and, even before she took her seat, said, "I have an answer to that question!" She sat down right away and began writing her journal entry. This question prompted a student-initiated discussion on world population and how a large population can be a detriment to society. One of the students even went over to a computer to look up population sizes of countries around the world. They were interested and motivated to find out more.

Sampson links the increase in her students' motivation to learn to the direct connection the big ideas have to her students' lives:

> I felt inspired; the big ideas were starting to have the effect I hoped they would. The students engaged with the material and began relating to it by inserting anecdotes from their lives. For example, during a discussion about governments and their effects on society, one of the students said her father was complaining about jobs going to China and how our government needs to do more to get jobs for Americans.

By using big ideas that push the relationship between past and present, students are more likely to make explicit connections to their own lives. Questions about stable societies and government influences are issues raised by historians, but they are also on the minds of people living today. History presented in these accessible forms empowers students to make better sense of the past and offers them an opportunity to see themselves as part of the bigger world.

A big part of helping students see a role for themselves is providing them with the tools and experiences that will enable them to make sense of the world around them. Mary Beth Bruce has her Advanced Placement students do a historiography workshop in which they learn about and assume the role of historian. Rather than being intimidated by the complexities of historical interpretation, her students embrace it:

> They were excited to hear that they were capable of interpreting primary, secondary, and tertiary documents, analyzing these writings,

synthesizing information, decoding vocabulary, comparing and contrasting historical schools of thought, drafting thesis statements, and crafting unique historical narratives. After two weeks of hard work, most of the students felt proud of their accomplishments.

In these several ways, the teacher-authors use big ideas as a way to leverage student interest in and engagement with the past. That interest and engagement may not pay off immediately in higher student test scores. But it is hard to argue that increasing the connections students make to history will disadvantage them on state-level tests.

More Student Voice

As more students connected more with the history they were learning, the teacher-authors found that their students' voices grew more pronounced in the classroom. Measuring student engagement with historical actors, ideas, and events can be challenging. In the cases of their teaching, however, the teachers focused on the character and level of discussion in their classrooms.

For example, Meyer discovered that he was talking less and his students were talking more:

> In past years I may have found that students were merely repeating something they had heard me say earlier in the unit, but this year I felt as though these ideas were their own responses and showed evidence of learning.

Like Michael Meyer, Julie Doyle noted that students ratcheted up their responses in the classroom dialogue when she refined her big idea questions:

> The open-ended big idea questions made the difference. When questions are too narrowly crafted, students' responses follow, as was the case where I directed the students to consider only native perspectives. I found that great, engaging discussions are possible with fifteen-year-old and sixteen-year-old students if, and only if, the students engage with the questions I pose.

Meyer and Doyle point to an important realization about teaching and learning: it is the students who need to demonstrate facility with ideas, not their teachers. Lecturing is a perfectly reasonable teaching method, but only if there are opportunities for students to demonstrate their emergent understandings.

Although it will surprise few readers to learn that students talk more in class if invited, the teacher-authors were surprised when their students' written responses also demonstrated elevated understandings. As Tricia Davis worked to improve her students' writing, she observed that when they are provided with open-ended big idea question prompts, they express themselves more fully:

> I am most gratified by these writing responses when a student's voice comes through like this. It reflects an ownership and an investment that I do not believe my students ever experienced when I assigned Regents essays. And as an added bonus, these responses are a treat to read! Each piece is unique; they are never formulaic. They make me laugh, they make me sad, as I feel the persona the student has adopted behind the writing.

Davis's students were better able to articulate their personal views when they responded to essay prompts that were more meaningful than the generic New York State essay prototype (also see Grant, Gradwell, & Cimbricz, 2004).

Employing a different outlet, Julie Doyle was happily surprised with the vivid responses her students offered during a blog assignment from a big idea question:

> Prior to reading her response, I had no idea that Laura held such passionate beliefs about world politics. I was similarly amazed at Matt's posting. . . . Like Laura, Matt rarely said much in class, but it was clear from his blog response that Matt held some very strong beliefs and that he felt comfortable sharing them so bluntly.

When history is rooted in a big idea approach, students seem better able to articulate their views rather than simply regurgitate information learned during a lecture or from a textbook. As Sarah

Foels notes, "they had a voice in what they were learning and they were proud of it."

CONCLUSION

In the sections above, we detail the several student-related benefits that the teacher-authors in this volume realized in pursuing big idea lessons and units. Those benefits, however, did not come easily or immediately. In the previous chapters, these teachers describe the tender negotiations they must sometimes engage in in order to teach the way they want. Karb and Beiter put it succinctly: "No worthy goal is ever reached without working around challenges that emerge; teaching is no different. In fact, knowing that these impediments exist is important, for that knowledge allows us to prepare and react accordingly." The teacher-authors encountered perceived and real contextual constraints, yet they navigated through them by using their rich disciplinary knowledge and deep understanding of their students to teach ambitiously in spite of the challenges.

NOTES

1. At the high school level, students must take and pass a grade 10 global history and geography exam and a grade 11 U.S. history and geography exam in order to graduate.

2. The RCT is a much simplified version of the standard Regents exam. Use of the RCT has declined significantly over the past several years, and the expectation is that it will eventually be phased out.

REFERENCES

Avery, P. (1999). Authentic assessment and instruction. *Social Education*, 63(6), 368–373.

Bain, R. (2000). Into the breach: Using research and theory to shape history instruction. In P. N. Stearns, P. Seixas, & S. Wineburg (Eds.), *Knowing, teaching, and learning history: National and international perspectives* (pp. 331–352). New York: New York University Press.

Baker, E. (1994). Learning-based assessments of history understanding. *Educational Psychologist, 29*(2), 97–106.

Barton, K., & Levstik, L. (2004). *Teaching history for the common good*. Mahwah, NJ: Lawrence Erlbaum.

Brophy, J., & VanSledright, B. (1997). *Teaching and learning history in elementary schools*. New York: Teachers College Press.

Cohen, D., & Spillane, J. (1992). Policy and practice: The relations between governance and instruction. In G. Grant (Ed.), *Review of research in education* (pp. 3–49). Washington, DC: American Educational Research Association.

Cornbleth, C. (2002). What constrains meaningful social studies teaching. *Social Education, 63*(3), 186–190.

Dewey, J. (1902/1969). *The child and the curriculum*. Chicago: University of Chicago Press.

Gerwin, D., & Visone, F. (2006). The freedom to teach: Contrasting history teaching in elective and state-tested courses. *Theory and Research in Social Education, 34*(2), 259–282.

Gradwell, J. M. (2006). Teaching in spite of, rather than because of, the test: A case of ambitious history teaching in New York State. In S. G. Grant (Ed.), *Measuring history: Cases of high-stakes testing across the U.S.* (pp. 157–176). Greenwich, CT: Information Age.

Grant, S. G. (2003). *History lessons: Teaching, learning, and testing in U.S. high school classrooms*. Mahwah, NJ: Lawrence Erlbaum.

———. (2005). More journey than end: A case of ambitious teaching. In E. A. Yeager & O. L. Davis Jr. (Eds.), *Wise social studies teaching in an age of high-stakes testing* (pp. 117–130). Greenwich, CT: Information Age.

———. (Ed.). (2006). *Measuring history: Cases of high-stakes testing across the U.S.* Greenwich, CT: Information Age.

———. (2007). Understanding what children know about history: Exploring the representation and testing dilemmas. *Social Studies Research and Practice, 2*(2), 196–208.

Grant, S. G., Gradwell, J. M., & Cimbricz, S. (2004). A question of authenticity: Examining the document-based question on the New York State global history and geography Regents exam. *Journal of Curriculum and Supervision, 19*(4), 309–337.

Kelly, T., & VanSledright, B. (2005). A journey toward wiser practice in the teaching of American history. In E. Yeager & O. L. Davis (Eds.),

Wise social studies teaching in an age of high-stakes testing (pp. 183–202). Greenwich, CT: Information Age.

Kohlmeier, J. (2005). The power of woman's story: A three-step approach to historical significance in high school world history. *International Journal of Social Education, 20*(1), 64–80.

Levstik, L., & Groth, J. (2002). "Scary thing, being an eighth grader": Exploring gender and sexuality in a middle school U.S. history unit. *Theory and Research in Social Education, 30*(2), 233–254.

Libresco, A. (2005). How she stopped worrying and learned to love the test . . . sort of. In E. Yeager & O. L. Davis Jr. (Eds.), *Wise social studies teaching in an age of high-stakes testing* (pp. 33–49). Greenwich, CT: Information Age.

Lortie, D. (1975). *Schoolteacher.* Chicago: University of Chicago Press.

McNeil, L. (2000). *Contradictions of school reform: Educational cost of standardized testing.* New York: Routledge.

Nuthall, G., & Alton-Lee, A. (1995). Assessing classroom learning: How students use their knowledge and experience to answer classroom achievement test questions in science and social studies. *American Educational Research Journal, 32*(1), 185–223.

Schweber, S. (2003). Simulating survival. *Curriculum Inquiry, 33*(2), 139–188.

Smith, J., & Niemi, R. (2001). Learning history in school: The impact of course work and instructional practices on achievement. *Theory and Research in Social Education, 29*(1), 18–42.

Smith, M. L. (1991). Put to the test: The effects of external testing on teachers. *Educational Researcher, 20*(5), 8–11.

Stevenson, R. (1990). Engagement and cognitive challenge in thoughtful social studies classes: A study of student perspectives. *Journal of Curriculum Studies, 22*(4), 329–341.

VanSledright, B., Kelly, T., & Meuwissen, K. (2006). Oh, the trouble we have seen: Researching historical thinking and understanding. In K. Barton (Ed.), *Research methods in social studies education* (pp. 207–233). Greenwich, CT: Information Age.

Vogler, K. (2006). The impact of a high school graduation examination on Mississippi social studies teachers' instructional practices. In S. G. Grant (Ed.), *Measuring history: Cases of high-stakes testing across the U.S.* (pp. 273–302). Greenwich, CT: Information Age.

Wiggins, G., & McTighe, J. (1998). *Understanding by design.* Alexandria, VA: ASCD.

Wineburg, S., & Wilson, S. (1991). Subject matter knowledge in the teaching of history. In J. Brophy (Ed.), *Advances in research on teaching* (pp. 305–347). Greenwich, CT: JAI.

Yeager, E., & Davis, O. L. (1996). Classroom teachers' thinking about historical texts. *Theory and Research in Social Education, 24*(2), 146–166.

10

IMPLICATIONS:
A ROAD MAP FOR
AMBITIOUS TEACHING
WITH BIG IDEAS

Jill M. Gradwell and S. G. Grant

In many ways, the preparation and completion of this book has been an extension of the work started by both authors' earlier studies. In a previous work, *History Lessons: Teaching, Learning, and Testing in U.S. History Classrooms*, S. G. Grant sketched out his initial ambitious teaching framework through the portraits of two U.S. history teachers, George Blair and Linda Strait. One reaction to the work was a review of the book in the Summer 2004 issue of *Theory and Research in Social Education* by Stephanie van Hover and Michelle Cude. In their review, they express their frustration with the lack of additional concrete examples of ambitious teaching to assist them in helping prepare their social studies teacher education candidates. After their students read the work as part of their course requirements, the students often asked, "But how do we do it [ambitious teaching]?"

We, too, shared similar frustrations when working with our own preservice and in-service teachers. Often, the teachers wanted exact recipes or step-by-step procedures for becoming an ambitious teacher. They wanted prepackaged lesson plans and curriculum units.

Even though we included in our methods courses "ambitious-like" teaching case studies, we faced skepticism, especially in light of the changes in state standards and assessments. For some, it was because we represent the academy and so must be too far removed from the classroom to really understand the day-to-day grind that teachers face. For others, the issue appeared to be the fear that ambitious practices may produce student failure in the classroom or on the state test.

We believe that ambitious teachers come in all shapes and sizes, and what our teachers really desired were more detailed examples of teachers like themselves, teaching in settings similar to their own working environments. Our preservice and in-service teachers wanted to hear from teachers who had to follow district-mandated curriculum maps, were pressured to emphasize test-taking strategies, or worked with challenging student populations. These concerns and others motivated us to pursue this project. We thought a collection of teacher-written narratives might bridge the gap between the classroom and the academy and be better received by teachers.

MAPPING OUT THE JOURNEY TO AMBITIOUS TEACHING

In chapter 9, we described the patterns and trends of the teachers in this book who are already on the road to ambitious teaching. Here, we map out some directions teachers may want to consider if they, too, want to be more ambitious. At heart, such teachers must first identify their strengths and weaknesses in the areas of subject matter, students, and context. Where they find areas in need of improvement, they must search for ways of enriching themselves.

FINDING WAYS TO INCREASE SUBJECT MATTER KNOWLEDGE

In some states, very little content knowledge coursework is required to hold a teaching certificate (Brown, 2006). Ravitch (2000) found in her study of the educational backgrounds of history teachers that less than half of the students enrolled in grades 7–12 history classes are taught by a teacher who at a minimum holds a minor in history. It is hard to imagine such teachers teaching ambitiously, as one of the key components is a strong understanding of the discipline.

That understanding includes both the substantive and syntactic structures of the discipline (Schwab, 1978). Knowing various historical narratives is only one part of the discipline (the substantive); recognizing that history is constructed, perspectival, and interpretive (the syntactic) is also key. To learn about and stay abreast of new historical understandings, teachers may want to take formal coursework in the area of history. However, taking courses at institutions of higher education can be costly and time consuming, two small luxuries teachers may not be able to afford.

Another avenue for teachers to increase their knowledge of history is to participate in the many public and private grant-funded professional development programs currently available. These projects may be sponsored by government agencies like the U.S. Department of Education, which funds the Teaching American History grant program. The National Endowment of the Humanities hosts programs for teachers such as Landmarks of American History and Culture: Workshops for School Teachers, the Picturing America School Collaboration Projects, and teacher summer seminars and institutes. Other professional development workshops are made possible through private or public nonprofit groups like the Gilder Lehrman Institute of American History and the United States Holocaust Memorial Museum.

Teachers can also stay current in their discipline by joining national professional historical organizations like the Organization of American Historians (OAH), American Historical Association (AHA), World History Association, and the regional and state affiliates of these groups. As a member of these organizations, you have benefits such as annual subscriptions to their flagship journals, opportunities to attend annual meetings and conferences, monthly newsletter subscriptions, and online networking to help you keep in touch with the state of the profession.

The subject matter knowledge teachers gain through such efforts cannot help but benefit their classroom instruction. That said, knowing one's content is not sufficient. As several studies have shown, strong history knowledge may be a prerequisite, but it does not ensure the ability to translate that knowledge into useful forms for children (van Hover & Yeager, 2003; VanSledright, 1996; Wineburg & Wilson, 1991; Yeager & Davis, 1996). As Shulman (1987) notes, teachers need to couple their deep content knowledge with a strong sense of their students, and thus develop pedagogical content knowledge.

LEARNING ABOUT ONE'S STUDENTS

Unsure of what students in general know and understand about history, teachers can look to the most recent theories and research in history education. Looking at the research base may shed light on how students make sense of historical documents (Barton, 1997; Foster & Yeager, 1999; VanSledright, 2002), multiple perspectives (Doppen, 2000), controversial issues (Hess & Posselt; 2002), or specific historical events (Levesque, 2003; Schweber, 2003). Teachers interested in finding out what students of different ethnic or racial backgrounds think about history may look to the work, for example, of Epstein (1998, 2009). For an exhaustive review of the relevant research literature, Barton's (2008) chapter in the recent *Handbook of Research in Social Studies Education* provides an excellent resource for teachers who are interested in students' notions of history.

Although much can be mined from reading about similar students in different settings, nothing can take the place of teachers researching and getting to know their own respective students. To do so is no easy endeavor. As a first step, teachers may want to immerse themselves in the school culture, not just that of the teacher's life but that of a student's too. Teachers can learn a lot about students through their extracurricular interests and by attending school events like athletic games and matches, band and chorus concerts, debates, school plays, and club functions. Teachers can also learn about the lives students lead outside of school by driving around the neighborhoods where their students reside, by meeting with school counselors and social service advocates responsible for their students' psychological and emotional well-being, and by inviting parents and guardians into classrooms.

Yet another way to learn about one's students is through classroom projects and assignments that encourage students to share pieces of their lives. For example, Jill Gradwell starts off one of her first classes with a postcard document-analysis activity. She provides color copies of a postcard she sent to her mother while teaching in Poland one summer. Without divulging any outside information about the postcard, she invites her students to interrogate the document to glean information about the writer, recipient, and events at the time. After a short class discussion about the nature of historical evidence, students make a list of possible artifacts that may be used by historians to construct an account of a person from the past. For homework, the students are asked to bring in an artifact from their own lives to be used in a similar activity during the following class. From the series of activities, students learn about the interpretive nature of history, and both teacher and students learn a bit about each other, fostering classroom community.

Teachers who know their content and students well may have sufficient pedagogical content knowledge (Shulman, 1987) to do good things in classrooms. Ambitious teachers, however, hold one additional form of knowledge: they understand the schooling context in which they teach. It is to that form of knowledge that we now turn.

FINDING CONTEXTUAL SUPPORT

One might think schools are places of considerable collegiality and support. After all, teaching is a complex and social process. Yet the egg-crate design of most schools, where teachers largely work out of sight of other adults, can lead to feelings of isolation (Lortie, 1975). School and school folks can also be actively discouraging, as in administrators who favor quiet classrooms over active learning, and testing programs that privilege low-level learning. Ambitious teachers, therefore, may not find much in the way of support for their ideas and practices. But that possibility is no certainty. Although Megan Sampson's experience stands as a cautionary tale of administrative abandonment, the teacher-authors did find support when they looked for it.

When teachers face what may seem like insurmountable barriers to engaging classroom instruction, the first place to turn may be department and school colleagues. Joseph Karb and Andrew Beiter are an excellent example of how two colleagues from the same department supported one another as they developed a rich historical unit. Sarah Foels and Mike Meyer also reported turning to other social studies teachers in their departments for help when developing units with big ideas. Although they found varying levels of assistance, those collegial conversations influenced how they approached their respective topics.

Teachers may find needed support in other departments within the school, as was the case with Tricia Davis. As she developed her "Culture Clash" unit, she collaborated with both the English language arts teacher and the living environment teacher to develop a curriculum about the Encounter era. And school administrators can be of help. Karb and Beiter found encouragement from their curriculum director after she suggested that they not be afraid to make courageous deletions of the core curriculum when organizing their teaching units.

If a teacher cannot find support within the school, there are other places to turn. Just as there are professional historical organizations like the AHA or the OAH, there are social studies/history education professional groups, like the National Council for the Social Studies (NCSS), National Council for History Education (NCHE), Society for History Education (SHE), and various regional and state councils. These groups, as well as others, can serve as a support for finding like-minded professionals dealing with current issues in history education. They have annual conferences, monthly newsletters, research branches, and online networks to facilitate teachers' pedagogical growth.

Casting the net even further, teachers may read about other examples of ambitious history teaching in academic and practitioner journals and books. For recent research and theory on history education, teachers may find the following journals useful: *Theory and Research in Social Education, Social Studies Research and Practice, Journal of Social Studies Research, International Journal of Social Studies Research, Journal of International Social Studies*, and *Contemporary Issues in Technology and Teacher Education*. For more practitioner-oriented examples, the most relevant journals are *The Social Studies, The History Teacher*, and the NCSS publications *Social Education, Social Studies and the Young Learner*, and *Middle Level Learning*. In addition to journal articles, a number of books (e.g., Grant, 2003, 2006; Stearns, Seixas, & Wineburg, 2000; Yeager & Davis, 2005) offer guidance on teaching history in a range of contexts.

THE COURAGE TO BE AMBITIOUS

A teacher may possess all the knowledge for being ambitious and still, at times, not act on it. This phenomenon continues to plague those interested in reforming teaching and learning. Barton and Levstik (2004) have suggested that when teachers can identify their purposes for teaching history, they are more likely to better align their practices and be more effective teachers. But they acknowledge that even teachers who know their purposes may or may not act on them. Barton and Levstik say they "have no magic formula" for encouraging teachers to push themselves, and they have a valid point.

However, based on the testimonies of the teachers in this book, one thing we have learned is that they share a quality that enables them to be ambitious: courage. Think back to each of the cases in this book. Although the circumstances varied considerably, each of the teacher-authors faced uncertainties and tensions as they went about their work. Unsatisfied with the status quo, these teachers possessed the courage to try something new—a new unit, a new form of instruction, work with a new student population.

Some were simply unhappy with how they taught in the past. Michael Meyer believed there could be a better way to teach about Africa. Tricia Davis envisioned a new writing approach for her students. Mary Beth Bruce wanted her students to engage in historical inquiry. All three knew, at some level, that there was a better way, and they had the courage to change their practices for the benefit of their students.

Others in the group were unsure of even where to begin to change their practices. Megan Sampson and Sarah Foels, both in their first years of teaching, had the courage to relinquish a measure of classroom control and allow their students to come to their own understandings. Julie Doyle had very little experience infusing technology into the classroom, but she did so as a way to foster more student engagement. Tricia Davis and Sarah Foels both faced new groups of students who came with new challenges. Rather than dumb down the curriculum, they continued to have high expectations for their students. As Davis suggests in her chapter, each of these teachers had the courage to take "a leap of faith."

We hope this book will inspire teachers to have the courage to ratchet up their practice despite the constraints they may be under. We would like to think that after reading about the ambitious teachers in this book, others might share the experience of one of our former graduate students. After she read a study about a teacher not unlike those represented in this book, she wrote in her reflective journal:

> After last night's class, I had an epiphany. For two years, I have been struggling with my constructivist philosophy about teaching and the New York State curriculum and assessment for 8th-grade social studies. All too often, I have found myself trying to balance authentic student-centered learning with attempts to cover the material in a timely manner. One day, I would be engaging students in a simulation of trench warfare and then the next go right back into lecturing or having students read from a secondary source. Not to sound insensitive to real medical conditions, but it was almost like I was a "bipolar" teacher. I would be happy and enthusiastic while engaging students in historical discovery, but I would be tired and less ani-

mated during more traditional teaching situations that covered the material. At times, I was so frustrated with the amount of information that the 8th-grade curriculum encompassed that I would come home from work and cry. As a nontenured teacher, I felt the weight of the final assessment crushing me.

Last night, after talking about what Sarah Cooper did in her classroom, I realized that I was sick and tired of trying to cram everything into one school year because of one test. All along, I just wanted to get students interested in the material and make my class more like an elective. I had small examples of what I wanted my classroom to be, but not the whole picture. I wanted more discussions, more authentic assessments, more documents, more persuasive and evaluative essays, more time for units, and more real-world learning experiences. I was unhappy and I was going to do something about it. Consequently, I came home from class and wrote out a proposal for my class, outlining what I was going to do differently and what I expected my students to do differently. This morning, I changed around the desks in my class to form a U-shape instead of rows. I told students that we needed to talk about something before going any further. I told them that I valued their ideas and interests and that I wanted us to share our learning experiences. I told them that there would be fewer pen-and-paper tests and more discussions, debates, simulations, document analysis, and group activities. I promised to teach them why the past was important and help them to be better people because of their knowledge. I let the real teacher inside of me take charge.

I don't know what will happen, but I do know that I am a much happier person right now. I am not going to let a test hold my creative energy back. Some students might resist, but I refuse to let them stop me. Even if kids fail the final assessment (which I do not think they will do because they will probably remember information better and be able to easily write DBQs), can the district blame me for trying to make kids connect to and appreciate learning more? If they do, then I don't want to work in that kind of environment.

We hope others will find the courage to be ambitious and to give teaching approaches like the use of big ideas a chance. But to do so, teachers must keep in mind that ambitious teaching is no walk in the park; it is challenging, nuanced, and highly contextualized work.

Teachers need to look for intersections of subject matter, kids, and context, and realize that, at times, these elements can conflict. In those instances, teachers will need the skills of negotiation and compromise, though always with an eye toward the greater goal of rich teaching and learning for *all* students. And as Sarah Foels points out in her chapter, "Wouldn't you be scared not to?"

MAPPING OUT THE FUTURE OF AMBITIOUS TEACHING

The cases presented in this book have implications not only for teachers but also for school leaders, policymakers, and researchers in the field of history education. Although it is true that schools are generally open enough to allow for a wide range of teaching practices, school administrators need to realize that ambitious teachers are the ones most likely to push forward the school's reputation. But to take best advantage of that expertise, administrators need to look hard at the organizational, logistical, and governance structures in the building to ensure that teachers are able to concentrate their efforts where they will be most useful—the classroom. We wonder, are there other ways school administrators might maximize teachers' time in lieu of dedicated "data days"?

Policymakers can also benefit from these cases. Tricia Davis's and Mary Beth Bruce's cases are both instructive in this area. Davis found that repeatedly using state testing prompts for classroom writing exercises stunted her students' growth in writing. After she started to use more authentic historical questions, she found her students' writing to be richer and more substantive. Similarly, Bruce moved away from the traditional test prompt and had her students develop their own theses about various historical themes. In both cases, when the teachers engaged their students with historical writing tasks modeled more closely after those that historians participate in, they found the level of student writing performance to improve. As we have argued in other work (Grant, Gradwell, &

Cimbricz, 2004), the New York State DBQ "offers students little in the way of an authentic historical experience" (p. 326) and "nothing in the way of a personal connection for students" (p. 327). State test-makers may want to consider replicating, on a larger scale, some of the writing tasks history teachers like Davis and Bruce are utilizing with their students if they are truly interested in moving toward a more authentic assessment of students' historical understanding.

Finally, the ambitious teaching examples in this book add to the history education literature that demonstrates the kind of teaching that is possible (Shulman, 1987) in schools under real and perceived constraints. More examples of empirical and conceptual research are still needed with teachers of other grade levels and in different kinds of settings. Possible research pursuits include the following questions: How do ambitious teachers develop their knowledge of the subject, learner, and context? How might teacher educators prepare teachers to be ambitious teachers? How does ambitious teaching impact students' understanding of history? More descriptive cases of ambitious teachers and teaching will provide a more nuanced understanding of what it means to teach history in schools today.

CONCLUSION

As we noted earlier, ambitious teaching offers no route to nirvana. The benefits to using big ideas to plan one's teaching units are several—more engaging content, more possibilities for instructional and assessment variety, and more opportunities to involve *all* students. That said, ambitious teachers do face challenges—the resistance of some students, the need to cut through a tangled curriculum, and the uncertain support evident by administrators. These challenges can seem daunting, especially to young teachers. Ambitious teachers know well their content, their students, and their particular school context. But they also hold a disposition to push themselves and their students in directions and toward goals that offer real possibilities for deep engagement with history.

REFERENCES

Barton, K. C. (1997). "I just kinda know": Elementary students' ideas about historical evidence. *Theory and Research in Social Education, 25*(4), 407–430.

———. (2008). Research on students' ideas about history. In L. S. Levstik & C. A. Tyson (Eds.), *Handbook of research in social studies education* (pp. 239–258). New York: Routledge.

Barton, K., & Levstik, L. (2004). *Teaching history for the common good.* Mahwah, NJ: Lawrence Erlbaum.

Brown, S. D. (2006). History teacher certification standards in the States. *The History Teacher 39*(3), 367–380.

Doppen, F. H. (2000). Teaching and learning multiple perspectives: The atomic bomb. *Social Studies, 91*(4), 159–170.

Epstein, T. (1998). Deconstructing differences in African-American and European-American adolescents' perspectives on U.S. history. *Curriculum Inquiry, 28*(4), 397–423.

———. (2009). *Interpreting national history: Race, identity, and pedagogy in classrooms and communities.* New York: Routledge.

Foster, S. J., & Yeager, E. A. (1999). "You've got to put together the pieces": English 12-year-olds encounter and learn from historical evidence. *Journal of Curriculum and Supervision, 14*(4), 286–317.

Gerwin, D., & Visone, F. (2006). The freedom to teach: Contrasting history teaching in elective and state-tested courses. *Theory and Research in Social Education, 34*(2), 259–282.

Grant, S. G. (2003). *History lessons: Teaching, learning, and testing in U.S. high school classrooms.* Mahwah, NJ: Lawrence Erlbaum.

———. (Ed.). (2006). *Measuring history: Cases of high-stakes testing across the U.S.* Greenwich, CT: Information Age.

Grant, S. G., Gradwell, J. M., & Cimbricz, S. K. (2004). A question of authenticity: The document-based question as an assessment of students' knowledge of history. *Journal of Curriculum and Supervision, 19*(4), 309–337.

Hess, D., & Posselt, J. (2002). How high school students experience and learn from the discussion of controversial public issues. *Journal of Curriculum and Supervision, 17*(4), 283–314.

Levesque, S. (2003). "Bin Laden is responsible; it was shown on tape": Canadian high school students' historical understanding of terrorism. *Theory and Research in Social Education, 31*(2), 174–202.

Lortie, D. (1975). *Schoolteacher.* Chicago: University of Chicago Press.

Ravitch, D. (2000). The educational backgrounds of history teachers. In P. N. Stearns, P. Seixas, & S. Wineburg (Eds.), *Knowing, teaching, and learning history: National and international perspectives* (pp. 143–155). New York: New York University Press.

Shulman, L. (1987). Knowledge and teaching: Foundations of the new reform. *Harvard Educational Review, 57*(1), 1–22.

Schwab, J. (1978). The practical: Translation into curriculum. In I. Westbury & I. Wilkof (Eds.), *Science, curriculum, and liberal education* (pp. 365–383). Chicago: University of Chicago Press.

Schweber, S. (2003). Simulating survival. *Curriculum Inquiry, 33*(2), 139–188.

Stearns, P. N., Seixas, P., & Wineburg, S. (Eds.). (2000). *Knowing, teaching, and learning history: National and international perspectives.* New York: New York University Press.

van Hover, S., & Cude, M. (2004). Ambitious teaching in an age of accountability. *Theory and Research in Social Education, 32*(3), 411–415.

van Hover, S. D., & Yeager, E. A. (2003). "'Making' students better people?" A case study of a beginning history teacher. *International Social Studies Forum, 3*(1), 219–232.

VanSledright, B. A. (1996). Closing the gap between school and disciplinary history? Historian as high school history teacher. In J. Brophy (Ed.), *Advances in research on teaching: Vol. 6* (pp. 257–289). Greenwich, CT: JAI.

———. (2002). *In search of America's past: Learning to read history in elementary school.* New York: Teachers College Press.

Wineburg, S., & Wilson, S. (1991). Subject-matter knowledge in the teaching of history. In J. Brophy (Ed.), *Advances in research on teaching: Vol. 2* (pp. 305–347). Norwich, CT: JAI.

Yeager, E. A., & Davis, O. L., Jr. (1996). Classroom teachers' thinking about historical texts: An exploratory study. *Theory and Research in Social Education, 24*(2), 146–166.

———. (Eds.). (2005). *Wise social studies teaching in an age of high-stakes testing.* Greenwich, CT: Information Age.

INDEX

Page numbers in italics refer to tables or figures.

ABOUT THE EDITORS
AND CONTRIBUTORS

S. G. Grant is the founding dean of the School of Education at Binghamton University. Previously, Grant was a professor of social studies education and an administrator at the University at Buffalo. He has taught middle and high school social studies in urban and rural schools in Maine and served as the state social studies consultant in the Maine Department of Education. He earned his PhD at Michigan State University. In addition to publishing papers in both social studies and general education journals, Grant has published four books, including *History Lessons: Teaching, Learning, and Testing in U.S. High School Classrooms* (2003) and *Measuring History: Cases of State-Level Testing across the United States* (2006). He won the Exemplary Research Award from the National Council for the Social Studies in 2004 for his *History Lessons* book.

Jill M. Gradwell is an assistant professor and coordinator of social studies education in the Department of History and Social Studies at Buffalo State College, State University of New York. She teaches both undergraduate and graduate courses in the teaching of history and research in social studies education and has been an educational consultant for five Teaching American History grant projects. She was a presidential fellow at the University at Buffalo, where she earned her PhD. Her research centers on teaching, learning, and assessing history and has been featured in such journals as *Theory and Research in Social Education* and *Social Studies Research and Practice.*

Andrew Beiter is a social studies teacher at Springville-Griffith Institute in Springville, New York, where he has team-taught a course on modern American history with Joe Karb. He has a BA in political philosophy from Michigan State University and a master's in education from Fredonia State College. Beiter was the national recipient of the 2007 Irena Sendler Award for Tolerance Education and a 2009 teacher fellow of the United States Holocaust Memorial Museum. He has run numerous workshops on the Holocaust and genocide prevention and is project director for the Summer Institute for Human Rights and Genocide studies in Buffalo, New York.

Mary Beth Bruce, a social studies teacher for the Sweet Home Central School District, teaches Advanced Placement U.S. history and a women's studies elective at the high school. She studied history and physical geography as an undergraduate at the University at Buffalo, where she also received her teacher certification for social studies 7–12 and master's degree in general education.

Tricia Davis is a global history teacher, Social Studies Department coordinator, and founding teacher at Tapestry Charter High School in Buffalo, New York. She has taught social studies courses in urban and suburban settings, including global history, participation in government, economics, and AP government. Her areas of research include teaching social studies with big ideas and teaching writing in the social studies classroom. She studied art history as an undergraduate and received a master's degree in social studies education 7–12 from the University at Buffalo. She received a regional mini-grant to develop curriculum around religious diversity and has presented on teaching social studies with big ideas at the New York State Council for the Social Studies conference and the national Expeditionary Learning conference.

Julie Doyle, a social studies teacher at Akron High School, teaches global history and geography Regents classes as well as participation in government. She taught at Bennett High School while working on her graduate degree. She received a BA from Loyola College in Maryland studying political philosophy and has a master's degree in adolescent education, social studies 7–12, from Canisius College. Prior to teaching, she gained experience in microfinance, grant writing, and nonprofit technology while living in Washington, D.C. In 2008, she coordinated a community-wide mock presidential debate to raise awareness of the major campaign issues and viewpoints of the candidates. Portions of the event were funded through a *History in Action*, a Teaching American History mini-grant.

Sarah Foels teaches grade 8 social studies in the Depew Union Free School District. She studied history and social studies education as an undergraduate at Canisius College and received a master's degree in social studies education 7–12 at Buffalo State College. In 2009, she presented on the topic of teaching with big ideas at the New York State Council for the Social Studies conference.

Joseph Karb teaches grade 8 social studies in the Springville-Griffith Institute Central School District. He studied social studies education at Buffalo State College, where he received a bachelor's degree, and at the University at Buffalo, where he completed a master's degree. He has served as a social studies instructional leader and has won awards from the Veterans of Foreign Wars and New York State United Teachers. He has presented on active learning in social studies and teaching about the Holocaust at several conferences, including the New York State Council for the Social Studies annual meeting.

Michael Meyer teaches history at the Clarence Central School District in western New York. He received a bachelor's degree in U.S. history from Harvard University in 1994 and a master's degree in social studies education from the University at Buffalo in 2007. He has also worked as a business executive in the field of technology consulting.

Megan Sampson is a global history teacher at the Charter High School for Applied Technologies in Buffalo, New York. She received a bachelor's degree in history from St. Bonaventure University and a teaching certificate and master's degree in secondary social studies education from the University at Buffalo. With her colleagues at the Charter High School for Applied Technologies, she worked to create a global history curriculum that has yielded high test scores and increased literacy for students in a developing district.